Voting Radical Right in Western Europ

The economic and political conditions that l
right parties exist in similar form and inte
radical right parties have only been succes
Germany, the *Republikaner*'s less than 2%
than the National Front's high of 15% and tl
the vote in national legislative elections. Why
of voters choose the radical right in Germany
winning more seats in Austria than in France
argument in this book is that radical right p
attracting voters and winning seats in electori
strategic voting and/or strategic coordination l
The analysis demonstrates that electoral systen
a key role in the success of the radical right.

Terri E. Givens is a professor in the governmen
versity of Texas at Austin. She has held fellowsh
dation and the European Union Center at the Un
She has conducted extensive research in Europe
Germany, Austria, and Denmark. Her articles l
parative Political Studies, the *Policy Studies Jou*
European Politics. She is an active member of
Science Association, the European Union Studie
Council for European Studies.

Voting Radical Right in Western Europe

TERRI E. GIVENS

University of Texas at Austin

CAMBRIDGE UNIVERSITY PRESS
Cambridge, New York, Melbourne, Madrid, Cape Town, Singapore, São Paulo

Cambridge University Press
40 West 20th Street, New York, NY 10011-4211, USA

www.cambridge.org
Information on this title: www.cambridge.org/9780521851343

First published 2005

Printed in the United States of America

A catalog record for this publication is available from the British Library.

Library of Congress Cataloging in Publication data

Givens, Terri E., 1964–
Voting radical right in Western Europe / Terri E. Givens.
    p.   cm.
Includes bibliographical references and index.
ISBN 0-521-85134-3 (hardback)
1. Elections – European Union countries.   2. Voting – European Union countries.
3. Right-wing extremists – European Union countries.   4. Political parties – European
Union countries.   I. Title.
JN45.G57   2005
324.2′13′094–dc22   2005000122

ISBN-13   978-0-521-85134-3 hardback
ISBN-10   0-521-85134-3 hardback

Contents

Acknowledgments

This book has been in process for many years, and there is no possible way I can thank everyone who had a hand in getting it to this point. However, I will make an attempt to briefly thank many of the people who have been instrumental in getting this project published. I'll begin by thanking my colleagues from my years at UCLA for their input on the project in its early stages, particularly Miriam Golden, Ron Rogowski, and Jim Denardo. I also would like to thank my colleagues at the University of Washington, particularly Adam Luedtke, Steve Hanson, and Margaret Levi, for their comments and advice.

A variety of scholars have provided guidance and support for this project. I thank Jeannette Money, Gary Freeman, Martin Schain, and the rest of the "immigration mafia" for their help over the years. Thanks to Neal Beck for technical assistance and to Kathleen Bawn and Jürgen Falter for providing some of the data for Chapter 4. Thanks also to Frank Lee Wilson for his assistance on Chapter 4.

Funding for this research was provided by the Center for German and European Studies and the Comparative Immigration and Integration program at UC Berkeley. My work in Denmark was supported by the European Union Center at the University of Washington. Patrick Weil of Centre d'Étude des Politiques d'Immigration, d'Intégration et de la Citoyenneté (Center for the Study of the Politics of Immigration, Integration and Citizenship) provided access to the library at Science-Po and office space during one of my stays in Paris. I am particularly grateful to the Max-Planck-Institut für Gesellschaftsforschung in Cologne, Germany, where I was able to perfect Chapters 5 and 6.

My European research could not have been successful without the help of scholars and students I met during my travels. I cannot mention them all here, but the resources of the Konrad Adenauer and Friedrich Ebert foundations were critical to my German research. Wolfgang Meixner, Peter Ulram, and Fritz Plasser were very helpful in Austria. In Denmark I received much assistance from the faculty of the Political Science Department at the University of Aarhus. Thanks to Frank Petrikowski and Pierre Martin for their assistance with my research and for their friendship.

Many people I met in my travels not only offered assistance with my research but also opened the doors of their homes. I thank the following people for their kind hospitality: the Bosc and Franco families, Kevin and Elisabeth Widrow, Tina Stausberg and Michael Pütsch, Klaus Brandenburg and Kirstin Neu, Pierre Martin, Frank Petrikowski, and Lilly Weber.

My family has been a major source of support during my years in graduate school. My parents, Rocelious and Leora Givens, gave me a strong foundation that allowed me to succeed in my academic pursuits. I dedicate this book in memory of my father. My sisters Marsha, Sharon, Rhonda, and Brenda were there with emotional support, and the occasional kick in the pants, when needed.

Thanks to Lewis Bateman at Cambridge University Press for his advice and help in getting to the final product.

Two of my greatest joys in life joined us on this planet while this manuscript was in preparation. Andrew and Brandon have brought more love and laughter into my life than I ever thought possible. Last, but most definitely not least, Michael Scott has been my main source of inspiration and love. He suffered along with me during the hard times and was my biggest fan during the good times. I can never thank him enough – but I'm happy to spend the rest of my life showing my gratitude.

Voting Radical Right in Western Europe

1

Introduction

1.1. THE PUZZLE

The dramatic entry of Jean-Marie Le Pen into the second round of the French presidential election of 2002 was a high point in the history of the *Front National* (National Front – FN) in France. This election was a clear challenge to "business as usual" in France. In the first round, Le Pen's 17% of the vote was a shock to then Prime Minister Lionel Jospin, who was only able to get 16% of the vote. Jospin was eliminated from what had been expected to be a second-round duel with President Jacques Chirac, who received 20% of the first-round vote (the lowest percentage ever for an incumbent). This election was one in which the two main campaigners were considered uninspiring and voters were faced with a choice of 16 candidates. These two factors led to a record high rate of abstention (28.4%) and allowed Le Pen to win second place with a small increase in vote share from what he had won in the previous election. Le Pen's advancement into the second round led to massive protests and a concerted effort by both the right and left to ensure that Chirac won the second round convincingly. Although many left voters held their noses as they voted, Chirac won the second round with 82% of the vote.

Le Pen's triumph in the presidential election was quickly followed by a disappointing but predictable result in the first round of the legislative elections. The FN received 11% of the vote, down from the 15% it had received in the 1997 election, and it did not win any seats in the French Assembly. Even in the 1997 election, the FN was only able to translate its 15% of the vote in the first round into one seat in the French Assembly. Although the FN has been considered one of Europe's most successful radical right parties, it has had difficulty translating the percentage of the vote it receives into electoral office at the national level.

After its success in the 1989 European Parliament elections, in which it received 7.1% of the vote, the *Republikaner* (REP) party of Germany looked forward to the possibility of gaining 5% of the national vote and entering parliament for the first time in 1990. Despite polls that showed that about 7% of voters were willing to vote for the *Republikaner*, the party received less than 2% of the vote in the 1990 legislative election and did not qualify for a seat in the German *Bundestag* (Lower House). The *Republikaner*'s loss was blamed on reunification and the downplaying of the immigration issue, as well as on the 5% electoral threshold that the party did not attain. The German *Republikaner* has been even less successful than the French National Front in winning seats in the national legislature.

In contrast, the Austrian Freedom Party (FPÖ)'s 27% of the vote in the October 1999 legislative election translated into 52 of the 183 seats in the Austrian legislature and dramatic entry into government as a coalition partner with the Austrian People's Party (ÖVP). The FPÖ has been the most successful radical right party in Western Europe. The party's leader, Jörg Haider, has been a controversial figure due to favorable references he has made to Nazi employment policies and his calls for a stop to immigration. His party's entry into government was followed by major demonstrations around the country and diplomatic sanctions from the 14 other European Union (EU) member countries.

The study of the rise of radical right parties in the 1980s and 1990s generally focused on economic and political change in Western Europe. The economic and political conditions that have led to the rise of radical right parties exist all over Europe. Unemployment was relatively high during this time and voters were beginning to show their dissatisfaction with the mainstream parties by either voting for new parties on the left and right or by abstaining. Yet, radical right parties have been successful only in a few countries. The *Republikaner*'s 2% of the vote is much lower than the National Front's 15% and the Freedom Party's 27% of the vote in national legislative elections. Arguments that rely on political and economic conditions to explain this variation cannot provide a complete picture. Why does such a small percentage of voters choose the radical right in Germany? Why is the radical right winning more seats in Austria than in France and Germany? To what extent can institutional differences, particularly those impacting party strategy, explain the contrasting electoral results?

Socioeconomic conditions certainly have played a role in the success of the radical right. The process of globalization has led to increased unemployment and increased uncertainty in industrial sectors of the economy. Blue-collar workers in particular have felt the brunt of the change to a more service-oriented economy. Immigrants often are used as scapegoats for unemployment. Many studies of the radical right have focused on two areas: (1) identifying changes in the political opportunity structure and identifying particular groups, such as blue-collar workers who choose to vote for the radical right (Betz 1994, Kitschelt 1995, Kriesi 1995); and (2) the relationship of aggregate socioeconomic variables to the vote for the radical right (Swank and Betz 1995, Jackman and Volpert 1996, Chapin 1997). These studies have provided valuable information on the makeup of radical right electorates and the motivations of different groups that vote for these parties.

What has been missing thus far in the literature is an analysis of the radical right that systematically compares the institutional structures, particularly electoral and party systems, in which these parties compete; widely divergent electoral fortunes show that socioeconomic conditions alone cannot explain differences in the success of radical right parties. To understand the variance in the success of radical right parties, one needs to take into account how different institutional settings affect the strategic behavior of both voters and parties.

I begin my analysis by replicating and building on the work of previous studies, comparing the types of appeals made by the radical right, the types of voters they attract, and the relationship of the radical right vote to unemployment and immigration at the regional level. My analysis indicates that these types of analysis cannot explain the causal factors behind the level of success of the radical right. I then examine the relationship among party systems, electoral rules, and the vote for radical right parties, taking into account the strategic interaction of the radical right with the mainstream parties. Through the use of statistical analysis and case studies, I show that strategic voting is a major determinant of a radical right party's vote and seat totals in an election.

My main argument is that radical right parties will have difficulty attracting voters and winning seats in electoral systems that encourage strategic voting by the electorate and/or strategic coordination by the mainstream parties. Strategic voting occurs when voters choose to vote for a party other than their preferred party because they are afraid of wasting their vote, or they are afraid that their least-favored party will win if they vote for their most-preferred party. Electoral rules may encourage strategic voting, but parties also can encourage strategic voting by signaling coalition preferences prior to an election or by indicating to voters that their vote for another party will be wasted.

Varying electoral rules and coalition structures provide different incentives for voters to vote strategically and for parties to coordinate on coalition strategy. These factors directly influence the ability of the radical right to attract voters and win seats. To support this argument, I compare the roles of strategic voting and strategic coordination in national legislative elections in France, Germany, Austria, and, in the final chapter, Denmark.

This study seeks to understand why individuals in similar socioeconomic environments choose to vote for the radical right in one type of electoral system yet not in another. The focus is on how individuals and parties respond to different institutional settings, while also considering the role of economic and social factors. Although the geographical focus is Western Europe, the analysis is designed so that the hypotheses can be applicable to other developed countries with multi-party systems.

The dependent variable throughout this study is the level of support received by the radical right in each of the four countries I study. The variable is measured through voting returns and seats won in national parliamentary elections. The percentage of support received by the radical right varies in each country, with the radical right receiving a higher level of support in France and Austria than in Germany. National-level electoral returns for each party are displayed in Table 1.1. The table shows that neither the National Democratic Party (NPD) nor the *Republikaner* in Germany have been able to get more than 4.3% of the vote in legislative elections. The National Front received 15% of the vote in 1997, and the Freedom Party received more than 20% of the vote in 1994, 1995, and 1999.

The main independent variables in the study are laid out in Table 1.2. Each of these variables has a positive or negative impact on the vote for the radical right in each country. I argue that there is little difference across countries in their ability to attract the "right kind of voter," who is basically the "modernization loser" as described by Herbert Kitschelt (1995) and Hans-Georg Betz (1994). The presence of immigrants and high levels of unemployment generally have a positive effect on the vote for the radical right, certainly not a negative effect. The main differences lie, and causal inferences can be made, in the variables related to strategic voting: the electoral system, coalition structures, and factionalism.

Chapter 2 focuses on the development of the radical right parties in France, Germany, and Austria. I argue that these parties can be considered

TABLE 1.1. *Percentage of the Vote Received by the Radical Right in Germany, Austria, and France: Legislative Elections*

Year	NPD/REP* 1st	2nd	FPÖ	FN 1st	2nd
1965	1.8	2			
1969	3.6	4.3			
1970			5.52		
1971			5.45		
1972	0.5	0.6			
1973				0.5	0
1975			5.4		
1976	0.4	0.3			
1978				0.8	0
1979			6.06		
1980	0.2	0.2			
1981				0.4	0
1983	0.2	0.2	4.98		
1986			9.7	9.7**	
1987	0.2	0.6			
1988				9.7	1.1
1990	1.7	2.1	16.6		
1993				12.4	5.7
1994	1.7	1.9	22.5		
1995			21.9		
1997				14.9	5.6
1998	2.3	1.8			
1999			26.9		

* NPD 1965–1987, REP 1990–1994.
** Proportional representation with one round of voting used.
Source: National election returns.

in the same category due to their nationalism and positions on issues such as immigration and the European Union. I begin by comparing different authors' descriptions of extreme or radical right parties and develop my own description of a radical right party, which focuses on the party's anti-immigrant stance and its self-portrayal as "outsider" in the party system. I then describe the radical right parties and their histories, including the factionalism that each party has experienced. Despite differences in their historical development during the 1980s and 1990s, the parties have taken very similar positions on key rallying issues like the presence of foreigners and resentment toward Brussels.

In Chapter 3, I present data that demonstrate the similarities between radical right voters in France, Germany, and Austria. Studies such as those

TABLE 1.2. *Factors Influencing the Success of Radical Right Parties*

	Attracting the "Right" Voters	Immigrants & Unemployment	Strategic Voting			Recent Votes*	Outcome Seats
			Electoral System	Coalition Structure	Factionalism		
France – National Front	+	+	–	–	–	11%	0
Germany – NPD and *Republikaner*	+	+	–	–	–	2.1%	0
Austria – Freedom Party	+	+	+	+	+	27%	52
Denmark – Progress Party and Danish People's Party	+	+	+	+	+	12%	22

* *Source:* National election returns.

by Kitschelt and Betz argue that the radical right has been successful because of its ability to win votes from modernization losers, or those who have lost out in the transition from a manufacturing-based economy to a services-based economy. I argue that survey evidence indicates that these parties have attracted these types of voters in all of the cases, regardless of a party's level of success. This type of analysis cannot explain differences in the success of these parties.

Many authors have examined the relationship among the number of immigrants in a country, unemployment, and radical right party success. Most of these studies have been done at the national level, which does not take into account regional variation, which can be an important factor in electoral success. In Chapter 4, I examine these variables at the district or regional level to determine their relationships with the vote for the radical right. Although these results do show that the radical right gets a higher percentage of the vote in regions where there are high numbers of immigrants and unemployment, they do not explain why this relationship exists in France and Austria but not in Germany.

The set of variables that I present next (the electoral system, coordination by the mainstream parties, and factionalism) influences strategic voting in an election. The electoral system plays an important role in determining the ability of a small party to gain votes. Electoral systems often are designed to make it difficult for small parties to compete, by the imposition of barriers such as electoral thresholds or requiring a certain number of signatures to be eligible for an election. Another way in which small parties are discouraged is coordination by the mainstream parties, which can encourage strategic voting. Factionalism in a small party also can lead to splits that can, at least temporarily, dampen support and discourage cooperation with more-mainstream parties. In Chapter 5, I develop the theoretical basis for strategic voting that will be analyzed in Chapter 6. I use the theories on strategic voting developed by Gary Cox (1997) and extend those theories by developing a model that includes a party's coalition signals to voters, which then influence strategic voting.

To extend the model into new terrain, I examine another case with a proportional representation (PR) electoral system. In Chapter 7, I apply my model to the Danish case. I chose Denmark because it has a relatively uncomplicated electoral system and party system compared with those of Austria and Germany. Denmark also allows me to examine a case in which immigration from developing countries has been a more recent phenomenon. Denmark is a strong test for my argument, since the socioeconomic conditions that other authors emphasize are not as strong in Denmark as in my other cases. The results in Denmark confirm my expectations that strategic voting (or lack thereof) is the key variable that channels potential radical right (RR) support into actual electoral success.

Research Design

This analysis does not discuss the *entry* of a radical right party into an electoral system – instead it is assumed that a radical right party has already been successful in entering the party system. In a study of party entry, Simon Hug (2001) has shown that ease of entry does not necessarily have an impact on the eventual success of a small party. The focus of this analysis is the factors that influence whether or not voters will choose to vote for an existing radical right party.

In order to maximize the system-level variables that can be controlled across cases, I use a "most similar systems" design, as formulated by Adam Przeworski and Henry Teune (1970). In this analysis, the cases chosen need to have systems in which the theoretically important processes exist, that is, multi-party systems where coalitions form and voters have the opportunity to vote strategically. However, it also is important to choose cases where the vote for the radical right varies.

Selection bias can be a problem in comparative analysis. Authors such as Barbara Geddes (1990) have pointed out the problems with making causal inferences when one selects on the dependent variable. The ideal situation would be to choose randomly from the universe of cases (such as all countries with multi-party systems), where the vote for (and seats won by) the radical right varies widely. However, as Geddes points out, "In practice, identifying the universe of cases that meet the structural criteria is probably an impossible task" (Geddes 1990, 144). This study attempts to balance the need for variance on the dependent variable with the need to study a few cases in depth. The cases need to vary on the dependent variable (percentage of the vote and seats won), as well as the main independent variables as shown in Table 1.2: electoral system, coalition structures, and factionalism. They also need to meet the main structural criteria (developed politically and economically, socially homogeneous) and be multi-party systems where coalition formation is an aspect of electoral competition.

I have chosen my cases from countries in Western Europe where a radical right party currently exists and has access to the electoral system.

Germany, Austria, France, and Denmark span a range of outcomes in terms of the electoral success of the radical right parties, unemployment levels, and the numbers of immigrants, particularly at the regional level. The NPD and *Republikaner* in Germany have never reached the 5% threshold required to enter parliament, while the FPÖ in Austria received 27% of the vote in the 1999 legislative election. The National Front in France received 15% of the vote in the 1997 legislative elections and 11% in the 2002 legislative elections. In Denmark, the Danish People's Party received 12% of the vote and 22 seats in the 2001 election. The cases also vary in their electoral institutions, with France using a single-member dual-ballot (SMDB) system and Germany a two-vote proportional representation system, while Austria and Denmark have a one-vote PR system.

These cases allow me to control for a variety of system-level social and economic factors. All of the countries are part of the European Union (with Austria joining in 1995) and the same "common market"; thus, similar economic factors are influencing the economies of each country. Each country has had significant inflows of immigrants since the importation of labor began in the 1950s (with Denmark having more recent flows). Despite an end to open labor recruitment in the 1970s, immigrant flows have continued due to family reunification, refugees, asylum seekers, and illegal immigration. These countries also have experienced similar economic difficulties, particularly rising unemployment rates during the transition to a service-oriented economy. The radical right in each country has tried to take advantage of economic discontent and the lack of solutions offered by mainstream parties, using immigrants as scapegoats.

What is important with the "most similar systems" design is that these cases are comparable, and they represent a range of outcomes to allow for generalization. The analysis will show that cultural issues and historical factors need not be invoked to understand the varying level of success of the radical right. Institutional factors, which vary across the cases, can be shown to influence the outcomes.

Rational choice theory underlies the main assumptions made in this analysis. I assume that parties are vote-maximizers, whether the goal is to enter government or simply to influence policies implemented by government. Parties and voters are constrained by the institutional structures that influence party strategies and voter choice. George Tsebelis points out that:

individual action is assumed to be optimal adaptation to an institutional environment, and the interaction between individuals is assumed to be an optimal response to each other. Therefore, the prevailing institutions (the rules of the game) determine the behavior of actors, which in turn produces political or social outcomes.   (Tsebelis 1990, 40)

This type of "institutional rational choice" (Dowding and King 1995) provides the framework for the analysis.

There are a variety of factors, such as Austria's grand coalitions, that make each of the electoral systems that I examine idiosyncratic.[1] To examine the model under a more mainstream type of system, I extend the model to the case of Denmark, which has structural and economic conditions similar to the three main cases. Denmark has a traditional PR system and also is a multi-party system. If the model holds for Denmark, I expect its outcome to be similar to the Austrian case. This will provide evidence that the general model is useful for understanding the rise of radical right parties in other countries.

In the following section I provide evidence that the radical right parties have similar levels of potential supporters yet varying levels of electoral success. I then review the comparative literature on radical right parties.

1.2. SUPPORT FOR THE RADICAL RIGHT

The level of support for radical right parties is only a puzzle if it can be shown that a party's support is higher than the percentage of the vote it actually receives. In this section I examine survey evidence and European Parliament election returns to determine if there is a baseline of support for the radical right. Although support for the radical right varies, I argue that each country has a set of voters who would be willing to support the radical right if it had a substantial chance of winning an election.

Underlying Baseline of Support

The small percentage of the vote received by the radical right in Germany may simply be an indicator that there is a lower level of support for the radical right in Germany compared with France and Austria. To determine

---

[1] Legislative coalitions made up of what are usually the two largest parties on the left and right are known as grand or great coalitions.

TABLE 1.3. *European Parliamentary Elections by Country (percentages)*

		Austria			
	FPÖ	ÖVP	SPÖ	LF	Greens
1996	27.6	29.6	29.18	4.23	6.8
1999	23.5	30.6	31.8	2.6	9.2

		Germany				
Year	NDP/REP	CDU/CSU	SPD	FPD	Green	PDS
1979	–	49.2	40.8	6.0	3.2	–
1984	0.8	46.0	37.4	4.8	8.2	–
1989	7.1	37.8	37.3	7.0	8.4	–
1994	3.9	38.8	32.2	4.1	10.1	4.7
1999	1.7	48.7	30.7	3.0	6.4	5.8

		France			
Year	FN	RPR/UDF	PS	PC	Greens
1979	1.3	43.9	23.5	20.5	–
1984	11.2	42.7	20.9	11.2	–
1989	11.7	28.9	23.6	7.7	10.6
1994	10.5	25.6	24.5	6.9	2.1
1999	5.7 (MN 3.3)*	35.1	22.0	6.8	9.7

* Movement National (National Movement) led by Bruno Mégret after split from LePen.
Source: European Parliament election returns.

the baseline level of radical right support, one can look at electoral support in local elections and survey results. In some cases, support may be evident in elections for the European Parliament because it is a pure PR system, and surveys have shown that voters don't take the election as seriously as national elections (and are thus willing to "waste" their vote on a most-preferred party). European and local elections are valid indicators of potential radical right support that can reveal if potential radical right support isn't being translated into real support in national elections. The results for these elections are displayed in Table 1.3.

Support for each of the radical right parties varies in European Parliament elections, but in at least some cases the parties have performed better in European parliamentary elections as compared with national legislative elections. The *Republikaner*'s best performance was in the 1989

European election, where it garnered 7.1% of the vote and representation in the European Parliament. After that election and unification, the radical right became more fragmented with the entrance of the DVU (*Deutsche Volksunion* – German People's Union) as a political party. However, the *Republikaner* still managed to get 10.9% of the vote (15 seats) in the Baden-Württemberg state election in 1992. Despite holding on to 14 of its seats in the 1996 state election, the *Republikaner* dropped below the 5% threshold in the 2001 state election, thus losing all its seats. In Austria, the Freedom Party also performed better in its first European election as compared with national legislative elections. The FPÖ received 27.6% in the 1996 European Parliament election compared with 21.9% in the 1995 legislative election. Although the Freedom Party's vote declined to 23.5% in the 1999 European election in June, its level of support increased again to 26.9% in the legislative election that October. The decline in the European election may have had to do with the Freedom Party's favoring Austria joining NATO, whereas 81% of Austrians favored staying neutral (Ignazi and Perrineau 2002, 175).

The French National Front received 11% of the vote in the 1984 European election compared with 9.7% in the 1986 legislative election. However, the National Front performed much better in the first round of legislative elections after 1986 than it did in European elections. For example, the National Front's result in the 1994 European election (10.5%) was worse than the percentage of the vote it received in the first round of the 1993 legislative election (12.4%). These results would indicate that the party's support is slightly higher in the first round of legislative elections than European elections. Voters have more parties to choose from in European elections in France, as compared with legislative elections where the mainstream left and right work more closely together, so the European elections may be less indicative of the FN's base of support than the first round of legislative elections.

Survey data also can shed some light on underlying support for the radical right. Veen (1993) reports that in spring 1989, "15 percent of West Germans were in favor of REP representation in the Bundestag and indicated that they might vote for REP candidates" (Veen 1993, 29). In a 1998 article, Viola Neu shows that while only 3% of those surveyed would vote for the REP or DVU, the percentage of those surveyed who thought it was a good idea for these parties to enter the *Bundestag* was between 11 and 18% in the previous five years (Neu 1998). Thus, there is evidence that the possible base of support for the *Republikaner* is higher than the percentage of the vote it has received in legislative elections alone would indicate.

Survey evidence indicates that the level of support for the FN is much more consistent over time than that of other radical right parties. In 1984, after the party's leader, Le Pen, appeared on national television, 18% of those surveyed "said they had a reasonable degree of sympathy with Le Pen" (Marcus 1995, 56). In a 1997 survey,[2] 20% of French voters stated that they agreed with Le Pen's ideas. The percentage of those who support the FN's positions is much higher than those who actually vote for the party.

In Austria, support for the FPÖ had declined to less than 2% prior to Jörg Haider's election as party leader in 1986. The party was able to attract more than 9% of the vote in the 1986 legislative election, and its totals have continued to increase over time. According to a quarterly survey published by the magazine *Profil* (Chladek 1997), the percentage of voters saying they would vote for the FPÖ if the election were held on the coming Sunday has ranged from 15% in December 1993 to a high of 29% in June 1997.

Support for radical right parties rises and falls over time, but overall support averages around 15% for the three countries. The main difference is that the level of support reported in German surveys does not translate into votes for the radical right, whereas in France and Austria the radical right parties have received between 15% and 27% of the vote. The survey results in particular make it difficult to argue that there is less popular support for the radical right in Germany than in the other countries.

If voters always voted sincerely, I would expect that the radical right in Germany would be receiving a higher percentage of the vote than they currently receive, given the percentage of voters who sympathize with the party. The fact that the German radical right gets a much lower percentage of the vote than its counterparts in France and Austria indicates that possible supporters of the radical right in Germany have incentives to vote for a party other than their preferred party.

1.3. COMPARATIVE WORKS ON THE RADICAL RIGHT

In this section I provide a brief survey of the literature that compares radical right parties in Western Europe. Existing works can be grouped

---

[2] SOFRES, *Local Press Group Survey*, March 5–7 1997, N = 1000.

into two "schools." The first set of authors, Betz (1994) and Kitschelt (1995), examine the radical right from an electoral behavior perspective. They focus on the idea that post-industrial capitalism has led to greater social fragmentation and "individualization" of risk, which has given the radical right parties the opportunity to attract voters who feel they are losing out in the current economic environment (modernization losers). The second set of authors (Swank and Betz 1995, Jackman and Volpert 1996, Lubbers et al. 2002) examines the relationship of socioeconomic variables such as unemployment and immigration to the radical right vote. Jackman and Volpert also take a first step toward examining the impact of an electoral system on the radical right vote, on which my analysis builds and extends.

One of the most comprehensive analyses of the radical right is Herbert Kitschelt's book, *The Radical Right in Western Europe* (1995). His main hypothesis is that "the success of the extreme Right is contingent upon the strategic choices of the moderate conservative parties as well as the ability of the extreme-rightist leaders to find the electorally 'winning formula' to assemble a significant voter constituency" (Kitschelt 1995, vii). Kitschelt argues that the combination of the strategies of the radical right parties and the closeness of the mainstream parties on the left-to-right spectrum determines which social groups will vote for a particular party. The main analysis describes how the parties' strategies attract particular groups of voters (those with "right-authoritarian" dispositions), using survey data and factor analysis. He finds that the success of radical right parties is dependent upon the type of issues they emphasize (authoritarianism, ethnic particularism, and market liberalism), which leads to the types of voters they are able to attract.

In a more descriptive analysis, Betz also uses survey data to determine the makeup of voters for the extreme right. He looks at how extreme-right parties' issue positions evolved from focusing on a liberal economic agenda to focusing on immigration and refugees. He notes that "a party's choice of strategy depends above all on which social groups it seeks to attract" (Betz 1994, 142). He argues that the extreme right's constituency became more and more blue-collar during the 1980s.

Both Betz and Kitschelt show that the radical right is attracting a particular type of voter in the countries that they analyze. These voters are typically male, young, and tend to be losers in the process of modernization. Betz's argument focuses on the similarities across countries of these modernization losers who are attracted to the radical right parties.

Kitschelt takes this type of analysis a step further and argues that the strategies of the parties are what make them attractive to the modernization losers. However, Kitschelt finds differences in the types of voters attracted to radical right parties in different countries. He finds that parties that are able to attract a broader range of voters are "populist" parties and not radical right parties. Radical right parties are therefore defined by their ability to attract mainly modernization losers.

Unfortunately, the survey data used in these studies are not always reliable and in the case of Kitschelt's analysis are limited to one year of data. A basic problem with studies that use survey data is the small number of radical right voters in a sample. For example, in a German survey the number of radical right voters may be 30 of 2000 respondents. It is difficult to obtain reliable results with such data. In the face of difficulties with survey data, several authors have turned to aggregate data analysis to determine the socioeconomic factors that are related to the success of radical right parties. These analyses focus on the relationship of factors such as unemployment or percentage of immigrants in a region and the vote for the radical right. Aggregate data are used to determine the effect of economic factors such as unemployment on the radical right vote. The basic hypothesis is that the radical right is more successful in countries or regions where the level of certain socioeconomic variables, such as unemployment or the percentage of immigrants, is high.

Within this second approach, Robert Jackman and Karin Volpert (1996) use aggregate data at the national level to test several hypotheses, including the effect of unemployment on the vote for the radical right. Their study also is one of the few to incorporate institutional variables. Their analysis includes variables for electoral disproportionality (the electoral threshold) and the effective number of parliamentary parties. Jackman and Volpert use a form of regression analysis (tobit) that allows them to include several cases in which the percentage of the vote for the radical right is zero. They expect to find that the level of support for radical right parties is higher in systems with lower electoral thresholds and higher numbers of parliamentary parties. Overall they find support for this hypothesis. They also find that "higher rates of unemployment provide a favorable environment for these political movements" (Jackman and Volpert 1996). These results indicate that the electoral rules as well as economic factors in a country may affect the support for radical right parties. Electoral thresholds are one part of an electoral system that may affect support for the radical right. However, Jackman and Volpert do not consider strategic behavior, thus their analysis of institutional factors lacks micro-foundations.[3] Their analysis does not analyze in detail why electoral rules may play a role, which is the focus of my analysis of strategic voting.

Duane Swank and Hans-Georg Betz (1995) conduct an analysis of the radical right using aggregate data at the national level in all 15 EU countries plus Switzerland. Their analysis includes variables related to trade openness and economic growth, as well as to foreigners and unemployment. Their results show that the vote for the radical right is positively related to variables such as per capita GDP and the inflow of asylum seekers. In the case of unemployment, they "find a positive, statistically significant effect of changes in youth unemployment rates on electoral support for [radical right] parties" (Swank and Betz 1995, 21). However, unlike Jackman and Volpert, they do not find a significant effect of general unemployment or electoral thresholds. These two studies suggest that unemployment is a factor in the level of success of the radical right, but it is not clear if this success is related to youth unemployment or general unemployment. The results for the role of electoral thresholds are contradictory, and clearly highlight the need for further investigation.

In a 2002 study, Marcel Lubbers and colleagues use large-scale survey data to explain what they describe as "extreme right-wing voting behaviour." They find that the number of non-EU citizens in a country does have an impact on the levels of extreme right-wing voting, but that unemployment has a negative, rather than the expected positive, effect. They also find that support is stronger in countries where anti-immigrant attitudes and dissatisfaction with democracy are stronger. The authors test the impact of political factors, including charismatic leadership, strong party organization, and active party cadres. They find that parties that have these characteristics are more likely to be successful. This study is very useful in that it combines individual-level data with contextual data from the 16 countries they study (EU plus Switzerland). However, the authors do not examine the nature of the party systems in which the radical right is competing, thus neglecting the impact of strategic voting in causing divergence between potential and actual RR support.

These authors have identified some factors that may influence the vote for the radical right, as well as indicate particular economic and

---

[3] Matthew Golder (2002) has criticized Jackman and Volpert's analysis and used their data to provide an updated analysis of radical right parties in Europe. As with Jackman and Volpert, his large-N analysis cannot factor in the role of party strategy and strategic voting.

social environments in countries where the radical right is successful. Unfortunately the results of these analyses often don't agree, so it is difficult to determine which factors actually affect the radical right vote. My analysis attempts to reconcile some of these contradictions and to consider carefully how institutional factors, particularly the strategic interactions between parties, influence voters and party strategy.

Although some of these analyses, particularly that of Jackman and Volpert, attempt to assess the impact of electoral systems on the vote for the radical right, they do not provide any systematic way of testing the combined impact of electoral systems and party strategy (particularly of the mainstream parties) on the radical right vote. Radical right parties do not exist in a vacuum. They compete on the same playing field as all the other parties in a party system. The institutional rules that define an electoral system and the way that parties react to those rules are critical to explaining differences in the level of these parties' success.

The analyses also generate unpersuasive conclusions because they too often remain at the macro level, ignoring the actions and decisions of real voters and real politicians. Thus, they cannot account for the way that voters choose a party. A rational choice model begins with assumptions that set up the context for an actor's choices. Using a model based on Cox's analysis of strategic voting allows me to factor in the way that voters strategize when voting. Voters are not mere automatons, reacting automatically to their socioeconomic conditions. Voters also care about potential electoral results, and they clearly avoid wasting votes on candidates whom they might actually prefer to those for whom they finally vote. I also incorporate the party side of the equation. Parties actively try to influence voters, not only through campaign materials but also by trying to constrain their choices and encourage strategic voting. A dynamic analysis that incorporates these party signals and voter choices can reveal the real political contestation that translates potential RR votes into real victories.

The analysis begins in the next chapter with a description of the radical right parties in France, Germany, and Austria. The history and positions of the parties are compared in order to lay the groundwork for the analyses in Chapters 3 through 7.

2

The Radical Right

2.1. INTRODUCTION

The rise of new parties on the right in the 1980s led to a great deal of controversy over how these parties are defined. Some authors argue that these parties share essential characteristics, while others point to the unique national features and circumstances of each party. Some see them as throwbacks to the fascist era, while others see them as mixing right-wing, liberal, and populist platforms to broaden their electoral appeal. The party ideologues themselves have argued that they cannot be placed on the left-to-right spectrum. In this chapter, I analyze the nature of radical right (RR) parties in France, Germany, and Austria. I argue that they can be considered in the same category due to their nationalism and positions on issues such as immigration and the European Union. These parties are aware of each other, so it is probable that they would emulate a similar party's success by evolving similar issue positions.

All of these parties also have experienced internal factionalism, which has threatened their success. As with many other types of parties, there are those within the party who would prefer to follow a more pragmatic path that might lead to greater electoral success, while other members are unwilling to change hard-line positions or pursue coalitions with other parties that might weaken ideological purity. In each case, conflicts between pragmatists and ideologues have led to major splits within the parties. The ability of a party to overcome these splits often has depended on the strength of the party leader.

It can be argued that one of the main differences among the parties is the ability of their leaders. For example, the parties in Austria and France have had leaders that are generally considered to be charismatic, which may have had a positive influence on the vote. However, the German parties have had difficulty finding a strong leader, which may have had a negative effect on their vote share. I argue that such strong leadership may help a party in its initial phases of development, but it cannot be measured directly. The basic problem with measuring charisma is that it can be tautological. Is a party successful because its leader is strong, or is the leader considered strong because the party is successful? In my analysis, the popularity and ability of a particular leader is only an important factor in holding a party together after a major split has developed.

In this chapter I examine the radical right parties' development, particularly in the context of each country's party system. I begin in the next section by comparing different authors' definitions of extreme or radical right parties, and I develop my own definition of a radical right party. I then describe the radical right parties and their histories in Section 2.3, drawing on interviews that I conducted with the radical right and the mainstream parties in each country. These interviews indicate how those on the radical right describe themselves, and how they are characterized by other actors in the political system. Section 2.4 provides a description of the nationalism that defines radical right parties and the positions they have taken on immigration, economics, and the mainstream parties. Despite differences in their historical development during the 1980s and 1990s, the parties have taken very similar positions on issues such as immigration and the European Union. In Section 2.5, I compare the leaders of each of the parties and their impact on the party's success. Section 2.6 concludes.

2.2. DEFINING THE RADICAL RIGHT

The rise of parties in Western Europe that generally have an anti-immigrant message has led to a debate on how these parties should be defined. In this section I describe the debate over what defines a radical right party and offer my own definition. Some authors refer to these parties as "extreme-right" and consider these types of parties to be anti-system (Ignazi 1992, Ignazi and Ysmal 1992, Fennema 1996). These authors tend to see these parties as a continuation of fascist tendencies that developed during the inter-war period and as anti-system in the sense that they are viewed as outside of, and challengers to, the mainstream party system. Others use terms such as "far right" (Cheles et al. 1995) or "new right"

(Minkenberg 1997) to describe the same set of parties, with an emphasis on the fact that these parties represent a new type of right party that had little or no connection to the fascist past. These differences in terminology are an example of the difficulty researchers have had in classifying these parties.

Despite varied labels, most authors agree that radical right parties do have certain characteristics in common. For example, Swank and Betz note: "Concretely, RRWP [Radical Right Wing Parties] combine radical free market programmatic commitments with xenophobic and strident anti-establishment positions" (1995, 1). In a survey of political experts by John Huber and Ronald Inglehart (1995), these parties (except for the National Democratic Party [NPD], which was not included) are placed on the extreme right. Although there may be different labels for these parties, they can be placed into a particular ideological category that is different from the center and far-left parties.

Rather than use terms like "extreme" or "anti-immigrant" that may have a negative meaning, I use the term "radical right" to describe the parties in this analysis. One of the main defining characteristics of these parties is their nationalism, which I describe in more detail. For the purposes of this analysis, radical right parties also have the following traits in common:

- They take an anti-immigrant stance by proposing stronger immigration controls and the repatriation of unemployed immigrants, and they call for a national (i.e., citizens only) preference in social benefits and employment ("welfare chauvinism").
- In contrast to earlier extreme right or fascist parties, they work within a country's political and electoral system. Although they do not have the goal of tearing down the current political system, they are anti-establishment. They consider themselves "outsiders" in the party system, and therefore not tainted by government or mainstream parties' scandals.

The specifics of these traits may change with time and the rise of new issues, but this description fits well for the radical right in the 1980s and 1990s.

Radical right parties are often compared to the fascist parties of the inter-war period. Authors such as Roger Eatwell (1995) and Michalina Vaughan (1995) have categorized radical right parties like the National Front and the *Republikaner* as "neo-fascist." According to these analyses, the anti-immigrant stances of these parties are one aspect of a neo-fascist political orientation. Of course, this type of classification is dependent on how one defines neo-fascism, but it is not clear that the term is an appropriate description for the current radical right.

Although there may be aspects of their party programs that harken to the past, there are clear differences in the historical contexts in which these parties and movements have emerged. Diethelm Prowe observes that one of the premier theorists on fascism, Roger Griffin, has argued that "fascist movements are destined to fail in modern 'liberal-secular' societies" (Prowe 1998, 306). Prowe himself has noted that there are similarities between inter-war fascism and present-day radical right movements, but he argues that they are "essentially different phenomena" mainly due to the historical context in which these movements have formed. The most important change he finds is the "transformation of Western European political culture...and the rapidly accelerating (re)emergence of a multi-cultural society" (Prowe 1998, 320). These factors have led to a radical right that relies on an anti-immigrant appeal. Although inter-war fascism did display a hatred of foreigners, Prowe argues that it was the "'broken society' of inter-war Europe" and class struggle that fueled the rise of fascism (Prowe 1998, 311).

A full comparison of inter-war fascism and the modern radical right is beyond the scope of this book, but it is useful to keep in mind differences in the electoral context in which these movements and parties have developed. Party systems, particularly in Germany, have been designed to avoid the kind of institutional rules that allowed the Nazi Party to gain a foothold in the Weimar regime. The present-day radical right parties have different institutional playing fields than the fascists of the inter-war period, which I will argue have contributed to their varying successes and failures.

2.3. PARTY BACKGROUND

In this section, I begin by describing the main political actors in France, Germany, and Austria. I then describe the history of the radical right parties in each country and my own encounters with the radical right.

During the spring and fall of 1997 I made several trips to Austria, France, and Germany to talk to strategists and politicians from the full range of parties in each country. The core questions in these interviews were designed to find out what the main issues of the day were in each country, how these issues were approached by the radical right versus the mainstream parties, the types of strategies the mainstream parties adopted for dealing with the radical right, and whether the radical right parties were willing to work with the mainstream parties.

I should note that as an African-American female I was generally well received, and I had few difficulties making contact with politicians and strategists within the various organizations. Most of the interviews were conducted in French and German, and all translations are my own. The main purpose of the interviews was to provide myself (a non-European) with a better sense of the context in which the radical right was developing. I also hoped to gain some insight about the strategies the radical right parties were pursuing, and the strategies that mainstream parties were using against the radical right. I have identified politicians and academics who were interviewed, but interviews with party strategists and staff were done anonymously. These interviews provide a snapshot of the parties and the strategies they were pursuing at the time. These strategies would later evolve, however, and are the focus of later chapters.

The Actors

I focus on the following radical right parties: the *Nationaldemokratische Partei Deutschlands* (National Democratic Party – NPD) and the *Republikaner* (Republicans – REP) in Germany, the *Freiheitlichen* (Freedom Party – FPÖ) in Austria, and the *Front National* (National Front – FN) in France. The *Republikaner* was founded in 1983, the NPD in 1964, and the FPÖ was originally formed in 1956. The FPÖ became more clearly identified with the radical right when Jörg Haider became the party leader in 1986. The FN was formed in 1972 with Jean-Marie Le Pen as party leader.

The mainstream political parties in Germany are the CDU (Christian Democratic Union) and its Bavarian branch, CSU (Christian Social Union), SPD (Social Democrats), and FDP (Free Democrats). The main parties in France are the Gaullist Rally for the Republic (RPR), the Socialist Party (PS), and the Communist Party (PC). The conservative Union for French Democracy (UDF) became an umbrella for several smaller parties in 1978. Austria has two main parties that have been part of government since the end of World War II. The ÖVP (Austrian People's Party) is the conservative, Catholic party, and the SPÖ (Social Democrats) represents the moderate left. The parties are displayed in their respective categories in Table 2.1.

TABLE 2.1. *Party Positions: Left to Right*

	Communist	Social Democrat	Liberal	Conservative	Radical Right
Austria		SPÖ	LF*	ÖVP	FPÖ
France	PC	PS		RPR/UDF	FN
Germany		SPD	FDP	CDU/CSU	NPD/REP

* The LF was formed in 1993 by a group of disaffected FPÖ members of parliament. The party is not included in the analysis.

The Freedom Party in Austria

The Austrian Freedom Party (FPÖ) was formed in 1956 and struggled for many years as a third party in a strong two-party system. From the party's inception in 1956 until 1983 it received between 5 and 7% of the vote in parliamentary elections. The party was made up mainly of German nationalists and those who pursued a liberal ideology, favoring lower taxes and less state intervention in the economy. The liberal side of the party dominated during the 1970s and up to 1986.

The FPÖ became a part of government in a coalition with the SPÖ in 1983 after the SPÖ lost its absolute majority in parliament. Inter-party rivalries, as well as a split between nationalists and liberals within the FPÖ, led to a collapse of the coalition in 1986. Nationalist Jörg Haider took control of the party after the power struggle in 1986. Haider has been outspoken in his anti-immigrant stance and German nationalism. However, the party's main strength was its ability to promote reform and attack the mainstream parties, particularly after a series of scandals involving politicians from the SPÖ and ÖVP. In 1993 the liberal wing of the FPÖ broke away to form a new party, the *Liberales Forum* (Liberal Forum – LF).

Austria has two main parties that have been part of government since the end of World War II. The ÖVP is the conservative, mostly Catholic party in Austria, and the SPÖ represents the moderate left. In 1947 the SPÖ and ÖVP formed a "Great Coalition" that lasted until 1966. The ÖVP formed a single-party government in 1966 that lasted until 1970, when the SPÖ was able to form a majority government. The SPÖ maintained a single-party government until 1983, when they formed a government with the FPÖ. This coalition fell apart in 1986, and the SPÖ and ÖVP once again formed a great coalition led by the SPÖ. This coalition would leave voters few options when discontent over economic policies began to develop.

Until the rise of Haider in 1986, the FPÖ had tried to improve its electoral fortunes through cooperation with the SPÖ. Norbert Steger, of the "neo-liberal" wing of the party, became party leader in 1980. Steger had helped to strengthen the liberal wing of the party, and the party was accepted into the Liberal World Union in 1979. Steger was successful in bringing the Freedom Party out of its electoral ghetto through the coalition with the SPÖ in 1983; however, the nationalist wing of the party was still an important force.

Brigitte Bailer-Galanda and Wolfgang Neugebauer (1997) point out that the FPÖ's state organization in Carinthia played an important role in maintaining the strength of the radical wing. Some of the more radical and nationalist members of the party came from this region. In 1983 Haider became the leader of the Carinthian Freedom Party, the largest state party group in Austria. The FPÖ had been represented in Carinthia's state legislature since the party was founded. It was this link with Carinthia that gave Haider the support to take over the party in 1986. Haider's move to directly attack both mainstream parties, as well as his move away from a liberal agenda, placed the party firmly on the radical right. Haider's populist stances, particularly on the immigration issue, increased the party's electoral success.

The FPÖ is well established at the local and national level. Some of the party's most impressive gains have been at the local level, such as in the Vienna council elections of March 2001, in which they won 20% of the vote. The party's base is in Carinthia, and it was unexpected that the party would have success in a region that was once an SPÖ stronghold. However, the FPÖ has become the strongest party in Carinthia.

Since 1986 the FPÖ and Haider have survived several scandals, including a scandal in 1998 that laid bare irregularities in the party's finances. Haider could no longer claim to have "clean hands," which had been his rallying cry against perceived corruption in the mainstream parties; however, his popularity did not decline significantly. The party was able to rebound from this scandal by early 1999.

In the October 1999 legislative election, the Freedom Party was expected to perform well, but the final outcome was not foreseen. The FPÖ received a slightly higher percentage of the vote than the ÖVP, taking over as the second-place party in Austria. The SPÖ received the highest percentage of the vote and attempted to continue the great coalition, but negotiations broke down after two months. The ÖVP formed a coalition with the Freedom Party, to the displeasure of the rest of the European Union (EU), as evidenced by shocked commentary from journalists and diplomats. The ÖVP's Wolfgang Schüssel took the position of chancellor, and Dr. Susanne Riess-Passer, Haider's top lieutenant, took the position of vice-chancellor in the newly formed government.

Haider eventually resigned as party chairman in order to blunt some of the criticism, but this did not stop the diplomatic sanctions that were imposed on Austria by the 14 other EU countries. The sanctions were eventually dropped after a group of Brussels "wise men" reported that Austria was not in violation of any EU accords.

After they entered government, support for the FPÖ declined significantly in opinion polls. Their first experience in government seems to have dampened some of the party's populist appeal. Haider continued to stir up controversy, meeting with Saddam Hussein in 2002, which led to his temporary resignation from the national party. Haider's continuing attempts to control the party members in government led to a crisis for the coalition and new elections in November. In that election, the Freedom Party only won 10% of the vote, although it eventually negotiated to continue its coalition with the ÖVP, which had substantially increased its vote total (42%).

Austria Interviews

My first interviews were with the Austrian Freedom Party in Vienna, and I also attended a party congress in Linz. My main interview was with Dr. Suzanne Riess-Passer in June of 1997 at party headquarters in Vienna. Dr. Riess-Passer at the time was considered to be second-in-command of the party behind Jörg Haider. In the interview, some of the main issues that she stated were important to the Freedom Party included the common European currency (which they felt should be delayed), illegal immigration, scandals within the Austrian government, and reducing government regulation and taxation. She also noted that the Freedom Party was able to break some Austrian political taboos, such as discussing the issue of international neutrality and the system of party privileges and patronage known as the "*proporz* system."[1]

Dr. Riess-Passer emphasized that the Freedom Party saw itself as neither right nor left and that the end of the cold war had brought an end to such right/left ideologies. The Freedom Party's desire to distance itself from an extreme right characterization also was evident at the party's annual congress in October of 1997 in which a video compared statements made

[1] See Chapter 6 for a discussion of the *proporz* system.

by Jörg Haider to similar statements made by left politicians such as Tony Blair, Bill Clinton, and Gerhard Schröder.

Since Haider took over the party in 1986 it was no longer willing to be a part of government at any price. The party wanted to have enough strength to have influence over government; otherwise it would use its influence as opposition. In another interview, the party's general secretary, Peter Westenthaler, discussed the future of the party in the fall of 1997, after the party's congress in Linz. He said that the party was preparing itself to become part of government and that it was likely to come in second after the SPÖ in the next election (his prediction would end up being correct). He stated that the party was willing to go into a coalition as a junior partner with either major party, as long as it was able to follow its program in government. It was partly this willingness to go into a coalition that I believe was an important factor in the Freedom Party's success in 1999.

Fritz Plasser, a political scientist and expert on Austrian political parties, made similar predictions about the Freedom Party in 1997. He felt that the Freedom Party would be able to win a higher percentage of the vote than the ÖVP in the next election. This would be a major change in the party structure of Austria, which had been a two and one-half party system since World War II. Plasser pointed out that the main reason for this change was a realignment of working-class voters. In the previous European election the Freedom Party had gotten the same percentage (45%) of blue-collar voters as the Social Democrats. Depending on the strategy of the Freedom Party and the Social Democrats, he felt that this would have a major influence on the outcome of the next election.

In comparison with other radical right parties, Plasser felt the Freedom Party compared most strongly to the French National Front. Both parties pursued similar issues and were able to attract working-class voters. They differed in that Haider often was inspired by politics in the United States. For example, he noted Haider's "Contract with Austria" was very similar to the "Contract with America" of the U.S. Republican Party. He also pointed out Haider's admiration for Bill Clinton's electoral campaigns. In comparing radical right leaders, Plasser stated that Haider and Le Pen are very different personalities. He contended that Le Pen is more of a traditional radical right leader, while Haider was better at media politics and performance.

Plasser noted that many voters felt that the Freedom Party was the only real opposition, despite the presence of the Liberal Forum and Green parties. Voters might choose the Freedom Party to send a message to the governing coalition. His research indicated that the Freedom Party was particularly attractive to younger voters who were tired of the current system and the scandals that developed out of it.

Interviews with strategists from the other main parties in Austria included the ÖVP, SPÖ, and Liberal Forum. In these interviews I confirmed the perception that the Freedom Party was considered to be to the right of the mainstream parties, despite the FPÖ's protestations to the contrary. It was interesting that strategists from the SPÖ and ÖVP each felt that the other party was showing indications of being willing to govern with the Freedom Party, and the SPÖ had even used this charge against the ÖVP in the 1994 election (this would end up being the case after the 1999 election). The ÖVP had tried to move toward Haider's positions on issues such as crime, drugs, and immigration, but it was wary of helping Haider by making these issues more mainstream. The party felt that voters would see the FPÖ as more legitimate if the mainstream parties were emphasizing the same issues. The SPÖ, which was leading the government at the time, had a new minister of the interior, Karl Schlögl, who was taking a hard-line, restrictive stance on immigration. It was felt that this was done to counteract Haider. Although the mainstream parties would have liked to simply ignore the Freedom Party, its increasing success made that impossible, particularly for the ÖVP. The responses to the challenge from the FPÖ included taking on its issues (particularly immigration), considering working with the party in government, and finding leaders who could try to match Haider's media appeal.

In general, my interviews in Austria highlighted the desire of the Freedom Party to build on its success by becoming a part of government. This desire was backed by a pragmatic side of the party, which was supported by Haider. Both of the mainstream parties were trying to influence public opinion regarding possible coalitions with the Freedom Party. These strategies helped me develop my hypotheses regarding party strategy and strategic voting that I examine in Chapters 5 and 6. The mainstream parties' approach to dealing with the National Front in the French case emphasizes the importance of institutions in the development of coalition strategy.

The National Front in France

The *Front National* formally became a party in 1972 and first contested elections at the national level in 1973. The FN performed very poorly in national elections during the 1970s and received only 0.35% of the vote in the 1981 legislative elections. The FN broke through in 1983 by gaining 17% of the vote in a local election in the town of Dreux, thus getting the attention of media across the country. The mainstream right joined a coalition with the FN on the second ballot in this local election, and the unified ticket won 55.3% of the vote, giving legitimacy and media exposure to the FN. In the 1984 European Parliament elections the FN won 11% of the vote and 10 seats in the European Parliament – the same percentage of the vote as the French Communist Party. In 1988 Le Pen received 14.4% of the vote in the presidential election and had an equally impressive showing in the 1995 presidential election. The FN received 9.6% of the vote in the first round of the 1988 legislative elections and 12.5% of the vote in the first round of the 1993 legislative elections.

The FN saw its best result in a legislative election in 1997. The snap election called by Chirac was a dismal defeat for the mainstream right parties. Chirac had hoped to consolidate his control of the legislature, but instead was faced with a rejuvenated Socialist Party, and his very unpopular prime minister, Alain Juppe, was unable to lead the right parties to victory (Ysmal 1998). In the first round of voting, the FN received 14.9% of the vote. Although 76 FN candidates were able to compete in the second round of voting, only one candidate was able to win a seat.

In terms of representation, the FN was more successful at the regional level, due to the proportional representation (PR) electoral system used for these elections. This highlights the impact of political institutions on the success of radical right parties. In the 1998 regional elections, the FN won 15.3% of the vote and gained many seats in the regional councils. This led to a crisis for the mainstream right parties, which had to rely on FN votes in several regions to be able to elect rightist regional presidents.

Subsequent to these successes, Bruno Mégret, a former RPR politician and considered to be Le Pen's heir apparent, began to push for more control of the party. Mégret was interested in forming coalitions with the mainstream right parties, but Le Pen opposed this strategy. The situation came to a head before the 1999 European election; Le Pen refused to put Mégret at the top of the list, and Mégret finally broke away and formed his own party (Ysmal 1999). In the European Parliament election, Le Pen's FN was able to get 5.7% of the vote and maintain its presence in the European Parliament, while Mégret's National Movement Party received 3.3% of the vote, which was below the national representation threshold.

After the 1999 European election, Mégret's party limped along, while Le Pen's FN worked to consolidate its position in anticipation of the 2002 national elections. The 2002 election was the first election after the presidential term was reduced from seven years to five years. It also was expected to be Jean-Marie Le Pen's last stand as the leader of his party. Le Pen stunned France and the rest of Europe by taking second place in the first round of the presidential election and qualifying for a runoff with President Jacques Chirac. After two weeks of anti–Le Pen protests, Chirac trounced Le Pen with 82% of the vote.

The FN hoped to gain some momentum from the presidential election, but its result in the first round of the legislative election was a disappointing 11%. The FN was able to field 37 candidates in the second round, but it did not win any seats. The mainstream right again refused to work with the FN, and this time its strategy worked. The RPR and UDF won an overwhelming majority of seats in the Assembly and controlled the executive branch and legislature.

France Interviews

When I conducted my interviews in France in 1997, the conflict between Le Pen and Bruno Mégret had not yet led to an open split between the two leaders. However, the beginnings of the split were clear to see. In that year's legislative election Mégret proposed to the UDF and RPR that they work together like the Socialists and Communists did to ensure that a right candidate would win a particular district. He argued that the FN was credible and capable of governing, as it had shown in the four cities where there were FN mayors.

In my interview with Mégret, he emphasized the role that immigration played in the recent election. He argued that illegal immigration was the most important issue for the electorate. He stated that the *sans papiers* (immigrants without papers) could not be assimilated and were causing problems for French society. He also stated that there was no ideological difference between the Socialists and the RPR. He felt that this lack of an ideological difference was a capitulation by the right in a country where there had always been a strong ideological debate. This would eventually lead to increased support for the FN. When asked about its electoral strategy, Mégret stated that the FN tried to show the electorate that the mainstream left and right parties were almost the same. Like the Freedom Party, the FN tried to show that it was the only real opposition party.

An interview with Mégret's cabinet director also emphasized the importance of alliances to Mégret's strategy. The director noted that the FN was becoming more important because it was increasingly able to enter the second round of the legislative elections, putting pressure on the right to work together in the second round. This had led to some alliances at the local level.

Interviews with strategists and party leaders from the mainstream right emphasized the distance these parties wanted to keep between themselves and the FN. Prior to 1997 there had been talk of a "Republican Front" against the FN. However, by the time I conducted my interviews this strategy had been discredited. It had given the FN more cause to say that the left and right were no different, that they were in fact working together. In an interview with an aide of the RPR MP from the town of Dreux, the aide emphasized that they would not go into a formal agreement with a left candidate to coordinate on the second round of the legislative election. They wanted to avoid becoming a "hostage to the left." He also noted that a part of the electorate didn't understand why the RPR and UDF couldn't ally with the FN, when the Socialists were willing to ally with the extreme left.

The UDF strategist I met with was very clear about the party's desire to avoid all alliances with the FN. He pointed out that the UDF's party leader had been much more direct in his denunciation of Le Pen and any collaboration with the FN than the RPR had been. It was from this interview that I first learned of the *Front Republicain* strategy against the FN during the 1980s. He noted that this strategy began in Dreux, where the Socialist, UDF, and RPR candidates agreed to work together to keep the FN from winning a legislative seat. However, he pointed out that this strategy became difficult because it made the FN appear to be the only opposition party. The strategy was thus abandoned, except at the local level.

My interviews in France emphasized the role that party strategy played in the success of the FN, as well as conflicts within the party. The mainstream parties' attempts at different strategies emphasized their fear that cooperation with the FN would lead to greater success for the party. The French case stresses the impact of institutions on electoral coalitions, since the two-ballot system put the focus of strategy on the actions of the parties in the first and second ballots, rather than trying to influence public opinion, as in the Austrian case. Avoiding cooperation with the FN seemed to be the main strategy during this time period, a strategy that was pursued more consistently against the radical right in Germany.

The NPD and *Republikaner* in Germany

It is important to note that Germany's history and aspects of Germany's constitution make the environment difficult for any radical right party.

Any party that is considered a threat to Germany's constitution can be banned, and parties such as the DRP (*Deutsche Reichspartei* – German Empire Party) were banned after World War II. Despite these factors, several radical right parties have managed to contest elections in Germany since the late 1950s.

The NPD (National Democratic Party) was formed in 1964 by several rightist regional parties, including members of the DRP, which had contested national parliamentary elections in 1953, 1957, and 1961. The NPD received only 2% of the vote in the 1965 parliamentary election but received enough votes to enter state parliaments in several *Länder* (state) elections from 1966 to 1969.

Splits began to appear in the party in early 1967. Two factions, one led by Adolf von Thadden and one led by Fritz Thielen, struggled for control of the party. The Thadden faction would win out, but the struggle caused difficulties for April 1967 state elections. Also, unemployment was declining, and the grand coalition that had been formed between the CDU and SPD in December 1966 was having success in both domestic and foreign policy. The NPD received only 5.8% of the vote and four seats in the state legislature of Schleswig-Holstein. The party received a slightly better 6.8% of the vote in Rheinland-Pfalz, but it only received four seats in the state legislature.

The NPD achieved its highest national-vote totals in the *Bundestag* election of 1969. The party nearly entered parliament with 4.3% of the vote in 1969 but fell short of the 5% of the national vote required to win a seat. When the economy began to improve in the early 1970s and the government stopped the importation of labor,[2] the party's support shrank, and the NPD virtually disappeared from the national electoral scene. During the 1970s the NPD made headway in the legislatures at the *Länder* level but was on the wane again by the beginning of the 1980s. The NPD still exists but has received less than 1% of the vote in recent years.

The German *Republikaner* was formed in 1983 by Franz Schönhuber and two other disgruntled members of the Bavarian Christian Social Union. After several years of infighting among the three founding members, Schönhuber, a journalist and former member of the Waffen SS, became party chairman in 1985. The name *Republikaner* was chosen in direct reference to the Republican Party in the United States – the party wished to be seen as conservative like Ronald Reagan (Veen et al. 1993).

---

[2] The percentage of foreigners nonetheless continued to increase due to family reunification, illegal immigration, and the flow of refugees.

The party received only 3% of the vote in the Bavarian *Land* (state) elections in 1986, but this made it eligible for federal electoral funding that allowed the party to organize throughout the country (Betz 1994, 18). In 1989 the *Republikaner* gained six seats in the Berlin *Land* parliament and six seats in the European parliament with 7.1% of the vote.

Despite the successes at the local level and in the European parliament elections, the *Republikaner* struggled at the national level. The party's best performances in national parliamentary elections were in the 1990 and 1994 *Bundestag* elections, where it received 2.1 and 1.9% of the vote, respectively. Although it has received more than 5% of the vote in Bavaria, the *Republikaner* has never achieved the 5% of the national vote necessary to gain seats in the national parliament.

The *Republikaner* has been distracted with internal quarrels, similar to those experienced by the NPD. The main disputes have been among party leaders. In 1990 Schönhuber quarreled with his own hand-picked successor and entered into a struggle for leadership of the Bavarian wing of the party. After a contentious party convention at which Schönhuber was reelected party chairman, he replaced his leadership team, and Dr. Rolf Schlierer became the new heir apparent. The party's internal struggles damaged its position in the eyes of the voting public, and the party barely missed making the 5% threshold in the Bavarian parliamentary election of 1990. The party rebounded in 1992 with 10.9% of the vote in the Baden-Württemberg parliamentary election.

The late 1990s saw a major decline in the *Republikaner*'s support at the state and national level. In 1996 the party only received 9.1% of the vote in the Baden-Württemberg state election, and in 2001 it dropped to 4.4%, losing its representation in the state parliament. The party was only able to get 1.7% of the vote in the 1998 *Bundestag* election.

The *Republikaner* is poorly organized outside of Bavaria and Baden-Württemberg, which has made it difficult for it to achieve success at the national level, despite some success in cities such as Berlin, Bremen, and Hamburg. Internal factionalization also has hobbled the party. In addition, as Nonna Mayer notes, it does not help that the party was put under surveillance by the federal constitutional court in 1992 and its members declared "right extremists" in 1995 (Mayer 2002, 309). Voters who may have already been hesitant to vote for a radical right party would be even less likely to vote for a party that was being considered a threat to German democracy. The party's decline is likely to continue, particularly since the CDU and CSU have been fairly successful at taking on the immigration issue.

Germany Interviews

My interview with the *Republikaner* in Germany revealed the extreme positions that the party was willing to take, even when talking to an African-American. I met with an advisor to the party's leader, Rolf Schlierer, in Stuttgart, where the *Republikaner* had 14 MPs in the state legislature (*Landtag*). One of the main concerns mentioned during the interview was with *überfremdung* (the proliferation of foreigners), which is considered by many to be a taboo term from the Nazi era. In particular, he emphasized the fact that Germany has a "Turkish problem" and that other nationalities don't play much of a role. He also noted that the *Sozialihilfe* (social welfare) received by an asylum seeker is more than what a German with five children receives. He argued that issues such as these and high levels of unemployment are why the *Republikaner* has been attracting the vote of blue-collar workers.

Schlierer's advisor did note, however, that the *Republikaner* viewed young, extreme right skinheads as idiots. He added that the media often linked *Republikaner* leaders with skinheads but that this was only due to a media bias. He complained about "political correctness" and the fact that one could no longer say the word *Neger* (Negro) while the word *Mohr* (Moor) was OK (a clear challenge to me as an African-American). He also argued that Germany should not have forgotten about Königsberg (aka Kaliningrad), formerly a part of East Prussia that became part of Russia after World War II. He stated that there were Germans still living there and that Germany had the resources to purchase the land. He also felt that World War II would not have happened if the Kaiser had remained in power after World War I. Many of the statements made by this strategist also were to be found in the party's newspaper.

We also discussed the *Republikaner*'s electoral chances now that Schönhuber was no longer a party leader. The advisor indicated that the *Republikaner* was hoping to build up support in the former East Germany, where they were working with another party in a few *Länder*. The party was having money difficulties because it had missed a filing deadline, but he noted that the FDP had missed the same deadline and had still received its state campaign funds. The overall impression I got from this interview is that the *Republikaner* (at least in Stuttgart) was made up of the more extreme elements of the party, now that Schönhuber and his supporters were gone.

My first interview with a mainstream party strategist took place in Munich in October 1997. I met with a leader of the SPD's youth organization for Bavaria, who also was a candidate for the 1998 national election. Bavaria was the main location for the RPR and the NPD party organizations. However, this strategist argued that the CSU had extreme elements and took on many of the themes of the extreme right, which kept the radical right from having any success in Bavaria: for example, the CDU and the CSU had taken on themes related to security and foreigner criminality, and parts of the CSU were anti-EU. He also pointed out that the *Republikaner* had no leader like Haider or Le Pen who was attractive to the public, and there also is a strong national consensus against the Nazis and neo-Nazi types.

The main strategy for dealing with the *Republikaner*, which was articulated by strategists from the Greens, SPD, FDP, and CDU, was to avoid giving the party any publicity or any special treatment. For example, in my interview with Otto Schilly (a SPD member of parliament at the time), he indicated that despite the *Republikaner*'s success in getting into some state legislatures, the best strategy was to ignore them and they would eventually show that they have nothing to offer. He also indicated that the CSU was able to stay on the far right to take away any place for the radical right in Bavaria. He noted that the press didn't pay much attention to the *Republikaner*, which kept them from gaining any publicity.

The FDP strategist I spoke with emphasized that the mainstream parties had learned from the debate over asylum policy in Germany and no longer allowed the radical right to dominate the theme of immigration. He felt that the themes in Germany were similar to those in Austria, however, so there was a potential for the radical right vote. The lack of a strong leader and the fact that the middle class wouldn't have anything to do with the NPD in particular kept them from gaining in strength. Unlike the CDU or the CSU, the FDP considered Germany a country of immigration and wanted a modernization of Germany's citizenship policy. He gave no indication that the FDP was likely to consider any kind of alliance with the radical right.

Peter Hintze, at the time the general secretary of the CDU, also indicated that the party leadership had forbidden any party members from working with the radical right. He stated that there was a clear consensus between the mainstream parties against the radical right. However, it was clear that the CDU also was willing to take a strong position on immigration. He stated that the CDU was against having an immigration law and noted that Germany had more immigration than all other European countries combined. They also were against changes to the citizenship law, which at the time virtually prohibited non-ethnic Germans from becoming citizens. He compared the CDU's positions to the more liberal positions of the SPD, which indicated that there were strong differences between the parties on these issues.

My interviews in Germany highlighted the mainstream parties' total unwillingness to even acknowledge parties like the *Republikaner* and NPD. This strategy seemed to be effective despite short periods of success by RR parties. The *Republikaner* clearly had become a more extreme party by the time of my interview, which lessened any hopes for cooperation with mainstream parties. Unlike the leaders I interviewed from the National Front and Freedom Party, the *Republikaner* was more willing to take extreme positions and less willing to play the "political game." The positions that these RR parties take may be similar, but there are differences in the extent to which they openly take extreme positions. This movement to the extreme by the *Republikaner* was at least in part due to the more extreme faction of the party taking control.

2.4. COMPARING PARTY POSITIONS

In this section I compare the radical right parties' positions on issues such as immigration, the economy, and the European Union. These positions are drawn from primary materials such as party programs, speeches, and interviews with party officials. I also draw from secondary sources, mainly books and articles that have explored the ideology of the radical right. To understand the positions that these parties take, one must first examine the nationalism that is a primary element of a radical right party's ideology.

One of the main defining features of radical right parties is their strong nationalism. Most of the positions that the parties take on other issues are derived from this nationalism. Ernest Gellner defines nationalism:

In brief, nationalism is a theory of political legitimacy, which requires that ethnic boundaries should not cut across political ones, and, in particular, that ethnic boundaries within a given state – a contingency already formally excluded by the principle in its general formulation – should not separate the power-holders from the rest.   (Gellner 1983, 1)

Therefore, any "foreign" presence is a threat to the nation as defined by the nationalist. Gellner goes on to point out that this nationalist principle is violated when foreigners are included in a nation or those who are considered nationals are not included. Nationalists not only want to exclude foreigners, they also may want to extend the actual territory of the nation to include those who are considered part of the nation.

For all of the radical right parties, the preservation of national identity is paramount. The radical right parties tend to see themselves as the only true "patriots" in the country. They claim that unlike the other parties in the country, they are not ashamed of the country's (wartime) history and long for a return to a more glorious past. This view can be seen in the way that party leaders in Germany and Austria downplay the Holocaust and Nazi crimes in World War II. In France, Le Pen also has downplayed the importance of the Holocaust, calling it "a detail of history." The party manifestos also provide evidence of their nationalist tendencies.

The Austrian Freedom Party's preamble to its October 1997 party program is entitled "Austria First." Melanic Sully notes that in this document

the party declared itself to be the only credible guardian of Austrian patriotism: "The Freedom movement puts Austria, the country and its people, above everything else especially party political interests."   (Sully 1997, 53)

Although the Freedom Party had been known for its German nationalism, the party has placed more emphasis in recent years on Austrian nationalism, while still acknowledging the common German cultural heritage.

In the 1984 European elections the National Front ran under the list name "*Les Français d'Abord,*"[3] highlighting the party's emphasis on French identity. The National Front, in the 1993 book *300 Mésures pour la Renaissance de la France,*[4] states:

The National Front is therefore in favor of a grand politics centered on national identity, aimed at the defense of our people, our cultural and natural patrimony as well as the values that make us what we are.   (Front National 1993, 23)[5]

The FN's leader, Le Pen, is well known for the oft-repeated statement, "France pour les Français!"[6]

The preamble of the *Republikaner*'s 1990 program begins with the statement: "Our Program is Germany" (*Republikaner* 1990, 2). The party emphasizes the German people's right to self-determination, in relation to the reunification of Germany. In my interview with a *Republikaner* official, it was clear that this reunification meant more than what had already occurred with the 1990 German reunification; it was clear that

[3] "The French First."
[4] *300 Measures for the Renewal of France.*
[5] All translations by the author.
[6] "France for the French!"

the party wanted to restore Germany to its 1937 frontiers, which would include expanding into Central Europe and giving Austria the right to reunite with Germany. These types of positions are more extreme than those of the Freedom Party or the National Front, but they tap into the German nationalism felt by many voters.

Immigration

Nationalism also guides the RR parties' positions on issues like immigration. Leaders of the radical right in Germany and Austria have declared that their homelands are not countries of immigration. In France, Le Pen has argued for the mass deportation of foreigners who threaten to overwhelm the "French" population with their numbers. Each of these parties has spoken out against a multicultural society.

The parties repeatedly relate unemployment and problems with law and order to immigration. For example, Le Pen regularly compares the number of unemployed French workers to the number of immigrants in the country. The assumption is that there would be fewer French unemployed if there were fewer immigrants. Jörg Haider has used the same formulation in comparing the number of *Gastarbeiter* (guest workers) to the number of unemployed in Austria.

The *Republikaner* includes immigration policy in the section of their 1990 party program dealing with law and order (*Republikaner* 1990, 13). For the most part, the *Republikaner* position on immigration is not much different from that of the CDU or the CSU. The difference comes during election campaigns, when the party is much more openly xenophobic. As Thomas Saalfeld points out, "In their public appearances, leading *Republikaner* politicians treat immigrants as scapegoats for unemployment, lack of housing and crime" (Saalfeld 1993, 191).

Immigrants are seen as a threat to national identity and the homogeneity of the country. In its 1993 party program, the Freedom Party states, "The protection of cultural identity and social peace in Austria requires a stop to immigration" (Sully 1997, 51). The issue of law and order arises again with the reference to "social peace." The party's position on immigration is outlined clearly in the 1994 electoral platform:

We [the Freedom party] stand for the preservation of natural ethnic groups and the protection of their cultural identity. However such protection is not to be extended to new immigrants. Austria is not an immigration country.

(quoted in Sully 1997, 52)

In 1992, the Freedom Party pursued a petition drive on an initiative that called for a stop to immigration. Entitled "Austria First," this initiative was ultimately unable to gather enough signatures to push the legislature to take any action. In the campaign for the initiative, the Freedom Party linked foreigners to crime and an increase in drug dealing.

In the French case, the National Front has been very clear over time about its position on immigration. The party's 1993 program begins with a section describing the dangers of continued immigration flows. The FN considers immigration to be "at the heart of the French crisis" (Front National 1993, 25). It also sees immigration as a danger to the civil peace and a major cause of unemployment.

Economic Policy

The common theme of the RR parties' economic positions is a contradictory combination of neo-liberalism on one hand and economic protection (particularly of the agricultural sector) on the other. For example, the *Republikaner* party has a positive attitude toward capitalism and neo-liberalism, but the party also appeals to more-insecure sectors of the middle, working, and agricultural classes with a call for anti-capitalistic protective measures. The 1990 party program emphasizes the role of the free market and private property in one section, yet calls for protection and state support of agriculture and small business in a separate section (Saalfeld 1993, 187).

Jonathan Marcus describes the FN's economic policy as follows, "The strong dose of economic liberalism often sits uneasily with the overarching demands of a politics of 'national preference.' The Front's policy seems to be torn between two poles – a sort of Francophone Reaganomics on the one hand, and nationalist corporatism or protectionism on the other" (Marcus 1995, 109). The 1993 party program calls for measures to support small and medium-sized companies. The FN also demands the protection of forests and agriculture, to allow for agricultural self-sufficiency for France.

The FPÖ's economic positions also are somewhat contradictory. Similar to the *Republikaner*, the party recognizes the need for private property but also calls for protection for agriculture. The 1994 party program states,

We want a competitive social market economy based on private property. We want the reduction of taxes and the privatization of all state-owned companies, administrative reform and a balanced budget.   (quoted in Sully 1997, 51)

But then it goes on to state,

We fight for the maintenance of the farming community through agricultural and forestry policies which guarantee the protection of agricultural structures and the maintenance of family farms. (quoted in Sully 1997, 52)

All of the RR parties defend farmers and argue for policies to protect the agricultural sector. Both the FPÖ in its 1997 program and the *Republikaner* in its 1990 program call for a "renationalization" of agricultural policy. This renationalizaton would protect the agricultural sector from collapse, as globalization progresses and competition increases from the East, as well as the West. The FN calls for a reestablishment of *la préférence communautaire* (community preference) that would no longer allow the entry of American agricultural products without tariffs (Front National 1993, 202). Marcus notes that the FN is willing to extend its idea of the free market to other nations within the EU, "on condition that the external barriers around its member states are sufficiently strong" (Marcus 1995, 110).

The positions of these parties have been described as "economic nationalism." Part of this economic nationalism is a rejection of the Maastricht Treaty and the European common currency. Each of the parties offers some minimal support for the idea of the European Union (more of a common market than a federal Europe), but they all question the way the treaties have been implemented and the bureaucracy in Brussels that they describe as having little accountability.

Attitudes Toward Mainstream Parties

The lack of responsiveness of the mainstream parties to the electorate is often a rallying point for the radical right. The radical right seems to strike a chord with some voters when they accuse government elites of not understanding the plight of the "common man." Each of these parties emphasizes that it is outside of the "corrupt party system." Although these parties do work within the system, they claim to be outsiders who have "clean hands," outsiders who are not a part of the many government scandals that have surfaced over the last few years.

Similarities and Differences

Although all of the parties emphasize the importance of strong families in their party programs, one of the differences among the FPÖ, the

FN, and the REP is the party position on the role of women (Givens 2004). The Austrian Freedom Party has little to say about women in its party programs. On the other hand, both the *Republikaner* and the FN are very strongly anti-abortion. The *Republikaner* also emphasizes that women and men are equal and should receive equal pay for equal work (*Republikaner* 1990). The FN argues that women should be given more opportunity to stay at home with their children (Marcus 1995).

There are small differences among the radical right parties, such as the positions they take on women. Each party must design a platform to fit its political environment. Although there are differences to be found in the party platforms of radical right parties, it is the similarities in the positions taken by these parties that are striking. It is likely that they learn from each other, through both direct and indirect communication. However, it also is clear that they are responding to similar economic and social conditions that make their positions appealing to particular segments of the population, on particular issues of high salience.

2.5. RADICAL RIGHT LEADERSHIP

Several authors have noted the importance of leadership to the success of radical right parties. As Lubbers et al. argue, "[P]eople are more willing to support candidates who mirror popular values than to support perceived losers" (2002, 352). In a broad cross-national analysis, they find that political factors, including having a charismatic leader, do increase the chance of a radical right party's success (Lubbers et al. 2002). In their study of the radical right in Scandinavia, Jørgen Goul Andersen and Tor Bjørklund (2000) argue that leadership is important in the early stage of a party's development. The cohesive leadership of the Danish and Norwegian Progress parties led them to be more successful than Sweden's New Democracy Party, whose leaders could not agree on strategy and ended up leaving the party. Christopher Husbands (cited in Andersen and Bjørklund 2000) also argues that the lack of charismatic leadership has had a negative impact on the radical right in the United Kingdom and the Netherlands. The radical right did have initial success in the Netherlands when a charismatic leader, Pim Fortuyn, appeared on the scene.

Of the parties described in this chapter, clearly the Freedom Party in Austria has had the most charismatic, albeit controversial, leadership. Jörg Haider is handsome, athletic, and an effective speaker. He is often on the cover of magazines, which show him climbing mountains or running marathons. Some Austrian magazines have clearly favored Haider, writing about him in a positive light. This portrayal is in contrast to Le Pen in France and Schönhuber or Schlierer in Germany, who have generally been portrayed negatively or not at all in the respective media markets.

Although the liberal wing of the Freedom Party broke away in 1993, this break actually enabled Haider to consolidate his control over the party. He no longer had to compete internally with the new leader of the *Liberales Forum*, Heide Schmidt, who had been another strong leader in the Freedom Party. Haider is credited with bringing more young people into a party that was beginning to age in the early 1980s. However, he has been able to maintain his relationship with many of the older members of the party. Although he stepped down as party leader after the 1999 election, he is still considered the main actor behind the scenes and has stated that he would consider running for chancellor in the next Austrian election.

Jean-Marie Le Pen also is considered to be an effective speaker and a charismatic figure for those who support the far right in France. Le Pen's strong leadership and control over his party led to its initial electoral successes in the 1980s. However, Le Pen has had problems with his temper, such as an incident in which he assaulted a female Socialist candidate during a campaign rally. He was convicted and eventually barred from holding office for one year.

Le Pen's problems, however, did not keep him from winning nearly 17% of the vote in the first round of the French presidential election in 2002. Although the actual number of votes he received did not increase significantly from the previous election in which he received 15% of the vote (4.6 million), a high number of candidates on the left, abstentions, and lack of support for Prime Minister Jospin propelled him into a runoff with President Chirac. The massive mobilization of votes for Chirac left Le Pen with only a slight increase in his votes in the second round (from 4.8 million to 5.5 million) and a resounding defeat.

Although Haider's party lost little support when the LF split from the Freedom Party, the opposite was true when Bruno Mégret split from the National Front. Mégret was able to take many of the more moderate FN leaders with him to his new party, which clearly hurt the FN in the 1999 European elections and the 2002 legislative elections. However, Le Pen's stunning second-place result in the presidential election of 2002 was the crowning success at the end of his career. The demonstrations that followed the first round of the election, and the media's complete denunciation of Le Pen, show the difficulty he faces compared with the relative media support Haider has received in Austria.

When the *Republikaner* elected Franz Schönhuber as party chairman, it was for the express purpose of having a leading figure who was recognizable to the public. However, Schönhuber could not win over many of the party activists, who did not appreciate his more pragmatic views. The *Republikaner* was then led by Rolf Schlierer, a rather colorless politician. Schlierer was unable to capitalize on *Republikaner* victories in state elections. He also has gotten very little positive media exposure in Germany, even less than Le Pen in France.

Neither Schlierer nor Le Pen have had the same type of support from the media that Haider has received in Austria, and neither cuts the same dashing figure that Haider does. Clearly, Haider himself has made an important difference in the success of the Freedom Party in Austria, as compared with the leadership of the National Front and the *Republikaner*.

Although there is clearly a difference in leadership, this factor alone cannot explain the difference in the level of success of the radical right, particularly when one looks at the number of seats that the parties have won in parliament. It is important to note that Le Pen's strength as a leader has not translated into seats in the French Assembly. Although it may be tempting to ascribe the Freedom Party's level of success to Haider's leadership and popularity, I will show in the chapters that follow that the strategy of the mainstream parties also played a role in the party's success. Party leaders are chosen on a variety of grounds – some are simply well connected, others are able to raise funds. Many small (and large) parties have less charismatic leaders who have not had an impact on the party's staying power.

2.6. CONCLUSION

The history of the three radical right parties described show that the 1980s and 1990s were a time of expansion for the radical right. This expansion was stunted for the *Republikaner*, despite taking positions similar to those pursued by the National Front and Freedom Party. This chapter has shown that there are clear similarities in policy positions that each of the parties has taken. There has probably been some cross-national learning among the parties. As one party has had success with an issue, another tries to replicate that success by taking on the same issue.

What is more difficult to replicate is party leadership. There are clear differences in the abilities and media portrayal of the parties' leaders. This leadership has varied across the three cases and appears to have played a role in the parties' initial success. However, leadership does not provide a full explanation of the variance in party success. In the next chapter I explore the issue of who votes for the radical right. Different social groups are drawn to parties for a variety of reasons. The success of the radical right also may be related to the types of voters they are able to attract.

3

Who Votes for the Radical Right?

3.1. INTRODUCTION

The puzzle to be explored in this book is why radical right (RR) parties have had more success in France and Austria (and Denmark) than in Germany. Chapter 2 introduced the radical right parties, showing that they have had varying levels of success in attracting voters, despite similar appeals. This chapter explores who votes for the radical right across the three countries. This type of inquiry has been central to the study of radical right parties in Western Europe. To understand why radical right parties have had increasing success in the last two decades, authors such as Herbert Kitschelt (1995), Hanspieter Kriesi (1995), and Hans-Georg Betz (1994) have studied the voters for these parties and the motivations behind the vote. Kitschelt also has looked at differences in radical right parties' constituencies to explain differences in these parties' levels of success.

The main argument in this chapter, however, is that *differences in who votes for the radical right cannot explain the difference in the radical right's level of success.* It is difficult to show systematically that differences in the level of success of radical right parties are caused by differences in the types of voters they attract. I argue that what is remarkable about radical right parties in Western Europe is not the differences in their electorates, but the similarities, no matter the level of electoral success.

To support my argument, I compare the electorates of radical right parties in France, Germany, and Austria during the 1980s and 1990s. I place the argument within the context of traditional cleavages, their effect on voting behavior, and the decline in the influence of these cleavages.

Although traditional cleavage structures have an influence on who votes for a particular party, this influence varies across countries and time. I demonstrate that there are few differences in the types of social groups who vote for the radical right across countries, when differences in the traditional cleavage structures and changes in the structure of the vote (e.g., Socialists losing their blue-collar constituencies) over time are taken into account.

The dependent variable in this analysis is the vote for the radical right in France, Germany, and Austria. The National Front (FN) in France and the Freedom Party (FPÖ) in Austria have had more success in attracting voters than the *Republikaner* (REP) in Germany. The main source of data in this chapter is national-level surveys, so the percentage of the vote is measured as the percentage of survey respondents who indicated they voted for a particular party. The independent variable is the social basis of support for each party that includes, for example, the percentage of blue-collar or white-collar workers who indicate that they voted for a radical right party.

In the following section I discuss different theories authors have used to explain the nature of the radical right electorate. I then describe in Section 3.3 general voting behavior and traditional cleavages in Austria, France, and Germany. In Section 3.4, I use national-level survey data to compare the radical right electorates. Section 3.5 concludes with a summary of the analysis.

3.2. LITERATURE ON THE SOCIAL BASES OF RADICAL RIGHT PARTY SUPPORT

Many analyses of the radical right vote simply attempt to describe the radical right electorate in a particular country. Authors who focus on a single country argue that the vote for the extreme right is mainly a protest vote against the mainstream parties (Mitra 1988, Mayer and Perrineau 1992, Westle and Niedermayer 1992). Hans-Joachin Veen and colleagues (1993) describe supporters of the *Republikaner* in Germany as disaffected from politics. Although some radical right voters use their vote as a protest, this does not explain why similar groups vote for the radical right in different countries. What the studies miss is the similarities in the electorates that can be found in a comparative analysis.

There are several studies that compare the electorates of radical right parties in Western Europe. Authors such as Betz (1994), Kriesi (1995), and Kitschelt (1995) use survey data to study the vote for the radical right. Betz (1994) focuses on the similarities between radical right voters, describing a new group of voters who are modernization losers. Kriesi (1995) compares the "extreme right" to the "new left" and finds that the ability to mobilize supporters in both types of social movements is affected by traditional cleavage structures and the responses of the mainstream parties. He also finds that extreme right parties have similar types of supporters. In contrast to Betz and Kriesi, Kitschelt (1995) has emphasized cross-country differences in the relationship between who votes for the radical right and these parties' level of success. His analysis of survey data indicates that voters for the FPÖ are different from those for the National Front or *Republikaner*. I will show that Kitschelt has overemphasized these differences, mainly because of changes that occur after the time period he analyzes.

In general, survey evidence indicates that radical right voters are predominately male, blue-collar workers or small business owners who have a low level of education. For example, Betz (1994) uses survey data from national election surveys and the European Union (EU)'s *Eurobarometer* to determine the nature of the parties' constituencies. Although he finds that these parties' constituents are not homogeneous, there are certain characteristics that do stand out. He finds that these parties are attractive to young men, the self-employed, and working-class voters (Betz 1994, 174). Betz shows that the makeup of the radical right's constituency became more and more blue-collar during the 1980s, as it changed its appeal from liberal economics to anti-immigration, to increase its following.

Kriesi finds that the radical right parties are attracting similar types of modernization losers. He argues that the difference in the parties' levels of success depends on the relative strength of traditional cleavages. The traditional cleavages, such as religion and class, restrict the ability of radical right parties to mobilize voters who may be attracted to their positions on immigration and economic change. He finds that traditional cleavages are weaker in France than in Germany and that this explains the difference in the radical right parties' level of success in these countries.

Kitschelt and Kriesi use survey data such as the *World Values Survey* and the *Eurobarometer* surveys to describe voters for the radical right. In the case of the *Eurobarometer*, data exist for all European Union countries. The 1990 *World Values Survey* used by Kitschelt includes data for countries from around the world. His analysis focuses on the following countries: France, Germany, Austria, Italy, Britain, Denmark, and Norway. As noted earlier, Kitschelt finds differences in the structure of the radical right vote in Austria, France, and Germany.

Kitschelt divides the radical right parties into four categories, based on the type of voters they should attract: fascist parties; welfare chauvinist parties; new radical right or right-authoritarian parties; and populist, anti-statist parties. Kitschelt argues that fascist parties draw their main support from small business, agriculture, and white-collar employees. Radical right parties draw support mainly from small business, agriculture, and blue-collar workers, while a populist party draws proportional support from all three categories (Kitschelt 1995, 35). A welfare chauvinist party receives support mainly from blue-collar workers. Kitschelt does not provide examples of a fascist or welfare chauvinist party in the cases he analyzes. The Austrian FPÖ and Italian Social Movement (MSI) provide examples of populist parties.

The French National Front is Kitschelt's prototype of a "New Radical Right" (NRR) party, while the German *Republikaner* is described as a NRR party that does not combine the right type of appeals. His "master case" is a radical right party that combines an authoritarian appeal with a capitalist appeal. He argues that a party with this type of appeal will find "the highest support among craftspeople, shopkeepers, and blue-collar workers" (Kitschelt 1995, 19). To test his hypotheses Kitschelt uses data from the *World Values Survey* of 1990. He begins by comparing the attitudes of voters for the radical right parties with those of the population (of the sample) in general. He finds that there are differences between radical right voters and what he calls populist party voters. Populist parties tend to attract voters from all occupational categories, while radical right parties tend to attract more blue-collar workers and the self-employed. Kitschelt cross-validates these data with *Eurobarometer* data that show that white-collar employees and professionals are underrepresented in both types of party, and that the populist parties have no distinctive occupational composition in their electorate. For example, in the case of Austria, he finds more equal support for the extreme right in all occupational categories.

Kitschelt's data in Table 3.1 display the percentage of each social group that votes for the radical right in Austria, France, and Germany in 1989. The main difference in the numbers is the percentage of highly educated voters who support the Freedom Party. In France and Germany the percentage of highly educated voters who vote for the radical right is much smaller compared with the other categories. Although Kitschelt would argue that this is due to the populist strategy of the FPÖ, I argue that this can be explained by the traditional cleavage structure in Austria. The Freedom Party has existed for a longer time than the other radical right parties and had both liberal and nationalist wings. It is more likely that it

TABLE 3.1. *Social Structure Supporting Extreme Right-Wing Parties – 1989 (in percentage of each social group)*

	Germany (REP)	France (FN)	Austria (FPÖ)
Occupation			
Self-Employed, Farmers	5.2	3.7	15.0
White-Collar, State Officials	3.3	2.4	9.0
Blue-Collar	6.3	3.3	Skilled 11.0
			Unskilled 8.0
Education			
Low	5.8	3.3	6.0
Medium	5.1	3.1	11.0
High	1.0	2.0	14.0
Gender			
Men	5.8	3.5	12.0
Women	3.1	2.2	7.0

Source: Kitschelt 1995, 77.

was the liberal wing of the party that attracted a portion of the electorate that is highly educated. I will show in Section 3.3 that once the liberal portion of the party had less influence, the profile of the party's electorate shifted to the less educated.

Kitschelt's analysis does not recognize the radical right's move away from the capitalist appeal, as described by Betz. Betz argues that the rise of the radical right coincided with governments' moves away from Keynesianism to a type of neo-liberalism, exemplified by the policies of the Thatcher government in Britain. The radical right adopted this neo-liberal approach, and the German *Republikaner* even chose its name to reflect its admiration of the American Republican Party and "Reaganomics." As socioeconomic conditions changed, the radical right began to abandon this neo-liberalism for a type of "economic nationalism." Although radical right parties started by pursuing a neo-liberal agenda, as economic conditions worsened in Europe, they began to change their strategy to attract those voters who felt threatened economically. Economic nationalism meant that these parties now promoted protectionist measures for sectors of the economy that were threatened by globalization and began questioning the governments' support of the Maastricht Treaty and the European Union.

A problem with both Kitschelt's and Kriesi's analyses is the static nature of the data and the fact that they are dealing with too few observations to make reliable inferences. Surveys such as the *World Values Survey* and the *Eurobarometer* surveys do not include enough radical right voters to get clear results, and they are limited to one or two years. For example, Kriesi's data from the 1990 *Eurobarometer* survey has only 41 respondents who indicated they voted for the French National Front and 10 who voted for the German *Republikaner*. Kitschelt's analysis using the *World Values Survey* is equally problematic, since it relies on data in which the radical right voters constitute only 4 to 9% of the national samples. In the case of Germany Kitschelt admits that "the results have to be taken with a grain of salt, as there are fewer than 30 Republicans in the entire sample" (Kitschelt 1995, 73).

To avoid the problem with such survey data, Betz uses national-level survey data to compare the voters for the radical right. Unlike Kitschelt and Kriesi, Betz does not attempt to use differences in the radical right electorates to explain the differences in their levels of success. Similar to Betz, I compare the results of national-level surveys; however, I am able to look at data from a longer time period to determine if differences in the radical right electorates can explain differences in their levels of success. To supplement the analysis in the German case, I use a method of ecological inference[1] developed by Gary King (1997) that can make inferences about individual patterns within group voting based on aggregate electoral and demographic data.

New Cleavages and the Radical Right

Authors such as Hanspieter Kriesi (1995) and Russell Dalton (1996) connect the rise of the radical right to the development of a new cleavage. Kriesi argues that the rise of the radical right has occurred due to a new cross-cutting cleavage that allows radical right parties to attract voters from both the right and left side of the political spectrum. This new cleavage is between those who have benefited from globalization and those who have either lost their jobs or whose jobs are threatened by globalization.

Although new cleavages may be developing in Western Europe, I focus on the continuing effect of traditional cleavages on party systems. Dalton (1996) describes the traditional cleavages as "Old Politics" and a new

[1] Ecological inference is a method used to infer individual-level relationships when individual-level data are not available. I describe the use of the method in relation to the German case in more detail in Section 3.3.

dimension as the "New Politics" cleavage. The Old Politics cleavage is based on the conflict between the "Old Left" working class and secular groups, and the "Old Right" business interests, middle class, and religious voters. The New Politics cleavage is based on new issues that have arisen in the last 20 years, such as environmental politics, minority rights, and social equality (Dalton 1996, 153). As Dalton points out, "The Old Politics cleavage is likely to remain the primary basis of partisan conflict in most advanced industrial democracies for the immediate future" (Dalton 1996, 153). More time is needed to determine if the radical right represents a part of the new cleavage described by Dalton and Kriesi.

Although it is not clear if a new cleavage is developing, there is evidence that the impact of traditional cleavages is declining. Increased electoral volatility and other indicators show that traditional cleavages are declining in their ability to predict voting behavior. In a different study, Dalton finds evidence for a decline in "social-based voting" in most categories, but particularly in class and religion (Dalton 1996, 328). This decline gives an opening to the radical right, but these parties must still contend with the ongoing, albeit weakened, influence of traditional cleavages.

If the traditional cleavages have a declining impact on the radical right vote, this decline may be seen in changes in the composition of the radical right vote over time. The time periods I focus on are the mid-1980s, when the parties first came to prominence, and the mid-1990s, when the parties were more established. The radical right may be attracting different types of voters, not only because their appeal may have changed but also because voters may feel less tied to parties that had represented their social group. The following analysis will be a test of a two-part hypothesis, partially drawn from Kriesi's analysis:

HYPOTHESIS PART 1: Traditional cleavage structures will limit a radical right party's constituency, particularly in the early stages of its development.

HYPOTHESIS PART 2: As the influence of traditional cleavage structures declines, the similarity of approach by parties in different countries will lead to the socioeconomic structure of the parties' constituencies becoming similar.

To test this hypothesis, I compare the vote for the radical right in the mid-1980s, when the parties were first coming into prominence, and the vote in the 1990s, when they had achieved success in France and Austria. Before moving on to this analysis, I examine the general makeup of the parties' constituencies and the declining impact of traditional cleavages.

3.3. CLEAVAGE STRUCTURES AND VOTING BEHAVIOR

This section begins with a brief survey of voting behavior and cleavages in France, Germany, and Austria. The studies discussed in this section focus on the social bases of the vote for particular parties. I focus not only on the role of traditional cleavages but also on the male and youth vote, where the radical right has shown strength.

Cleavages and the Mainstream Party Vote

The traditional cleavages described by Seymour Martin Lipset and Stein Rokkan (1967) are class, religion center-periphery, and urban-rural. Until the 1970s, voting behavior in Europe was dominated by these same cleavages, which had dominated party systems since the 1920s, leading Lipset and Rokkan to describe the West European party system as "frozen." The traditional cleavages divided the party system into the socialist left and conservative right in most countries.

Since 1970, the entrance of new parties, in particular Green parties, challenged the idea of a frozen party system. Authors such as Dalton (1996) and Inglehart (1990) argue that the importance of new issues, such as the environment, led to "issue voting." For example, Green parties were able to attract voters by focusing on specific environmental issues such as nuclear energy. Despite these findings, other authors, such as Mark Franklin and colleagues (1992), argue that traditional cleavages still play an important, although declining, role in voting behavior.

In France, Germany, and Austria there is evidence that traditional cleavages continue to play a role in voting behavior. Cleavage structures are similar in these countries. For example, conservative parties in Western Europe are linked to traditional religious groups. This is particularly true in the case of the Christian Democratic Union and the Christian Social Union (CDU/CSU) in Germany and the Austrian People's Party (ÖVP). Social democratic parties in France and Germany tend to attract blue-collar workers and younger voters.

Cleavages have been particularly strong in Austria, where the party system has emerged from the three *Lager* (camps) that developed at the end of the nineteenth century. The Social Democrats (SPÖ) represent the Socialist camp and have attracted the blue-collar workers' vote. The conservative ÖVP represents the Catholic-conservative camp[2] and has generally received a large share of its vote from the middle class and farmers. The

[2] The ÖVP is generally considered the successor party to the CSP (Christian Social Party) but tried to recast itself as a new party after World War II.

FPÖ represents the German-national camp[3] and has mainly attracted German nationalists across the range of social groups.

The traditional cleavage structures in Austria still have some influence on the vote for each of the parties, but changes have occurred over time. For example, the SPÖ has traditionally been supported by blue-collar workers, but support from white-collar workers also has been strong, although it is declining (Plasser et al., 1996). The ÖVP remains the favored party for farmers and those who are religious.

German voters are similar to Austrians in that blue-collar workers tend to vote for the Social Democrats (SPD), and the Christian-conservative side of the cleavage is represented by the CDU/CSU. Unlike the SPÖ, the SPD in Germany continues to attract a higher percentage of blue-collar workers than white-collar workers. Religion also continues to play a role in the German electorate. The Christian Democrats (CDU/CSU) generally poll more than 50% of the Catholic vote. The *Republikaner* is new to the party system, and it is not yet clear if it represents a new cleavage.

A high percentage of Catholics also tend to vote for the center right Union for French Democracy (UDF) and the Gaullist Rally for the Republic (RPR) parties in France. In a 1989 survey, 70% of regularly practicing Catholics stated that they had voted for the center right. Blue-collar workers tend to support the Socialist (PS) and Communist (PC) parties. As with the *Republikaner*, the FN is a new part of the party system and does not represent a particular traditional cleavage. The FN attracts both practicing and non-practicing Catholics, as well as blue-collar and self-employed workers.

The decline in the impact of traditional cleavages is considered generally to have been a continuing process since World War II. This process became more apparent with the rise of Green parties in the 1970s and 1980s. A simple way of examining this decline is to look at the change in the vote for those parties that represent the traditional cleavages. Table 3.2 displays the percentage of the vote received by each party from the early 1980s to the mid-1990s and the change in the vote for the mainstream parties. The table indicates that since the early 1980s the combined vote for the mainstream parties has declined in each country.

The most significant changes in the combined vote of the mainstream parties have been in France and Austria. In 1983 the two main parties in Austria received 91% of the vote. By 1994 this total had dropped to 63%. In France the three main parties dropped from 93% to 59% from

---

[3] Those who believe Austria and Germany should have closer ties, or even be reunited.

TABLE 3.2. *Change in the Vote for Mainstream and Radical Right Parties, Percentage of the Vote Received in Legislative Elections*

			Austria			
Year	SPÖ	ÖVP	Total	Change	FPÖ	Greens*
1983	47.7	43.2	90.9		4.98	4.2
1986	43.1	41.3	84.4	−6.5	9.7	5.9
1990	42.8	32.1	74.9	−9.5	16.6	8.5
1994	34.9	27.7	62.6	−12.3	22.5	7.31

* From 1983 to 1990 there were several Green parties.

France (1st Round)

Year	RPR/UDF	PS	PC	Total	Change	FN
1981	40.1	36.3	16.1	92.5		0.2
1986†	44.8	30.7	9.8	85.3	−7.2	9.7
1988	37.7	36.4	11.3	85.4	0.1	9.7
1993	39.7	17.3	9.2	66.2	−19.2	12.4
1997	23.4	25.6	9.9	58.9	−7.3	14.9

† PR system used in this election, only one round contested.

Germany (2nd Vote)

Year	CDU/CSU	SPD	FDP	Total	Change	Green	NPD/REP‡
1983	48.8	38.2	7.0	94		5.6	0.2
1987	44.3	37.0	9.1	90.4	−3.6	8.3	0.6
1990	43.8	33.5	11.0	88.3	−2.1	3.8	2.1
1994	41.5	36.4	6.9	84.8	−3.5	7.3	1.9

‡ NPD 1983–1987, REP 1990–1994.
Source: National election returns.

1981 to 1997. The difference in Germany has been much smaller. In 1983 the three main parties received 94% of the vote. By 1994 that total had dropped by less than 10% to 84.8%.

Since most analyses of cleavages focus on class voting, I focus on this category to determine change in the class structure of the mainstream party vote. The mainstream parties in Germany appear to maintain their constituencies, despite indications that class voting is weaker in Germany than in France and Austria.[4] The survey data in Table 3.3 indicate that there has not been a major change in the makeup of the constituencies

[4] Dalton (1996) uses data from the 1990–1991 *World Values Survey* to determine Cramer's V correlations to test the strength of class voting in Western democracies. Germany has a correlation of .13, France .15, and Austria .20.

TABLE 3.3. *Germany 1987 and 1994 Legislative Elections, Percentage of Social Group by Party*

	Green 1987	Green 1994	SPD 1987	SPD 1994	CDU/CSU 1987	CDU/CSU 1994	FDP 1987	FDP 1994
Gender								
Male	7.7	10.2	41.3	40.4	42.6	38.8	7.0	5.1
Female	6.8	12.4	39.3	42.3	45.5	37.3	7.0	4.5
Education								
Primary	2.0	5.4	51.9	46.4	38.8	40.6	4.9	2.9
Secondary	8.7	11.8	38.6	40.2	41.1	38.7	8.5	4.8
University or Higher	15.1	20.7	34.3	34.0	36.0	33.2	12.6	8.0
Profession								
Farmers	0	4.4	15.0	15.3	79.6	71.5	5.3	3.6
Self-Employed	3.6	10.3	20.9	22.9	61.6	52.8	11.8	9.3
Managers, Professionals	8.4	11.2	33.6	39.8	45.8	40.1	10.4	5.9
White-Collar	7.9	13.0	37.5	40.9	45.1	37.1	8.3	5.0
Blue-Collar	4.0	6.8	52.6	51.5	37.4	33.8	4.5	2.0
Age								
18–24	23.4	18.4	38.3	36.7	28.9	32.4	7.3	5.9
25–34	14.8	18.0	43.0	44.5	33.3	27.7	6.7	4.5
35–44	5.8	15.4	45.5	44.3	39.5	30.4	8.0	4.9
45–59	1.3	6.9	43.9	40.4	46.5	43.4	6.9	5.4
60–69	1.0	4.0	40.8	39.5	49.0	49.5	7.1	3.7
≥70	0.3	1.8	37.7	35.9	55.0	55.0	5.4	4.4
TOTAL*	6.7	11.3	42.1	41.3	42.6	38.1	6.9	4.8
N	601	1114	3806	4074	3846	3754	625	472

* Percentage of voters who stated they would vote for the specified party in the next election.
Source: Forschungsgruppe Wahlen 1995. *Politbarometer West [Germany], 1977–1995 Partial Accumulation,* 1987 data N = 10,000, 1994 data N = 10,000.

of the mainstream parties, although they are getting a smaller overall percentage of the vote. For example, the SPD still gets more than 50% of the blue-collar vote, the CDU/CSU continues to get a high percentage of the self-employed and farm vote, and the FDP also gets a high percentage of the self-employed.

Table 3.4 indicates that the PS in France has experienced a fairly large drop (12%) in the percentage of blue-collar workers voting for the party. This drop is part of an overall decline in each category; however, the percentage of blue-collar workers is the largest decline. The RPR/UDF actually increased their share of most social groups, *except blue-collar*

TABLE 3.4. *France 1986 and 1997 Legislative Elections, Percentage of Social Group by Party (unweighted results)*

	PC 1986	PC 1997	PS 1986	PS 1997	RPR/UDF 1986	RPR/UDF 1997
Gender						
Male	7.7	13.9	41.6	33.0	40.7	29.8
Female	7.1	11.7	44.0	30.6	40.6	34.4
Education						
Primary	8.3	13.7	43.4	30.8	40.1	34.4
Secondary	5.8	13.1	37.0	32.4	45.1	28.9
Vocational or Technical	9.5		42.6		36.8	
University	5.2	11.7	43.7	32.0	43.2	33.0
Profession						
Farmers	0.5	3.1	25.2	20.8	71.4	70.8
Self-Employed	4.4	9.0	31.4	20.7	50.4	58.6
Managers, Professionals	6.3	9.2	41.9	33.7	44.0	45.3
White-Collar	6.7	11.0	44.6	37.4	39.2	41.1
Blue-Collar	12.5	16.4	50.9	37.6	46.4	33.0
Age						
18–24	7.9	14.2	49.5	32.9	25.0	29.2
25–34	8.2	13.4	44.2	34.5	34.9	24.4
35–44	8.3	14.4	47.5	38.9	36.6	20.0
45–54	7.2	13.4	39.2	30.1	45.2	25.7
55–64	7.7	13.1	37.6	28.8	48.6	31.3
≥65	5.5	9.5	40.6	26.4	47.1	45.0
TOTAL	7.4	12.8	42.8	31.8	40.6	37.5
N	214*	257	1233	640	1171	648

* Number of respondents who stated they voted for this party in 1986 or 1997.
Sources: SOFRES *Post-Electoral Survey*, May 1988, N = 3000; SOFRES, CEVIPOF *Post-Electoral Survey*, May 1997, N = 3000.

workers. The Communist Party also increased in each category under professions.

The vote for the Austrian mainstream parties also has dropped significantly, so I would expect to see major declines in each of the categories. Table 3.5 indicates that the SPÖ has managed to maintain its hold on blue-collar voters, while the ÖVP has had a significant decline in this category. Both parties have lost white-collar workers and managers. One of the biggest declines for the ÖVP has been with the self-employed. They also have lost strength with farmers, one of their main traditional bases of support.

TABLE 3.5. *Austria 1986 and 1994 Legislative Elections, Percentage of Social Group by Party*

	Green 1986	Green 1994	SPÖ 1986	SPÖ 1994	ÖVP 1986	ÖVP 1994
Gender						
Male	4	5	42	34	38	25
Female	5	9	43	36	43	30
Education						
Primary	3	3	47	45	42	28
Secondary	3	4	45	50	38	24
University or Higher	11	16	29	19	46	32
Profession						
Farmers	1	0	1	8	93	73
Self-Employed	6	8	14	10	60	40
Managers, Professionals	6	8	49	35	33	23
White-Collar	7	7	57	29	36	25
Blue-Collar	4	2	49	47	27	15
Age						
30	11	12	39	31	33	19
31–44	6	11	43	31	37	26
45–59	1	5	42	37	48	30
≥60	1	2	45	41	44	33
TOTAL	4.9	7.3	43.1	34.9	41.3	27.7

Source: Plasser and Ulram 1995, 356 and 358.

Survey data cannot indicate which voters are switching to different parties, but it is clear that the mainstream parties in France and Austria (with the exception of the French PC) are losing parts of their traditional constituencies. These declines over time would support my hypothesis that traditional cleavages may be weakening over time, although in the Austrian case one party may have suffered more than another from the decline. I explore next in more detail whether this has had an impact on the radical right vote.

Gender and Age

Gender has not been considered a traditional cleavage, but it does play an important role in the radical right vote. In Europe, the mainstream parties generally have a higher percentage of women in their electorate than men, in part because women are about 52% of the electorate and men are about 48%. For example, in Austria the SPÖ and the ÖVP each have a higher percentage of female voters (around 54%) than male voters (around 46%). The percentages are similar for the SPD and CDU/CSU in Germany, with the percentage of women around 53% and the percentage of men around 47%. This also is the case for both the Free Democrats (FDP) and the Green Party in Germany. Results from a survey after the 1995 French presidential election indicate that the conservative and socialist candidates' voters were about 52% female and 48% male. These percentages are in stark contrast to the radical right parties' voters, who tend to be closer to two-thirds male and one-third female (Givens 2004).

Another factor in the radical right vote, which I discuss in more detail next, is the disproportionate percentage of young voters in their constituencies. The mainstream parties tend to get a disproportionate share of votes from older voters. In general, young voters tend to abstain in higher numbers or vote for more progressive or new parties.

Radical Right Voters

Each of the radical right parties has been accused of xenophobia and of using fear to attract voters. The fact that each of these parties has used immigration as a major rallying issue shows that they are trying to appeal to voters who feel threatened by immigration. These voters also feel threatened by economic change, in general. Although these parties have used different appeals at different times, they are generally seen as attractive to a particular type of voter. I employ here the evidence that other authors have used to determine the type of voter the radical right is attracting.

A major change occurred in the FPÖ after Jörg Haider took control of the Freedom Party in 1986. The FPÖ was no longer considered a liberal party, but closer to the extreme right. Anton Pelinka and Fritz Plasser's (1989) analysis of FPÖ voters from 1982 to 1986 shows that the party still had support from its traditional base of highly educated and older voters. In this analysis, Pelinka and Plasser conclude that the Freedom Party's electorate had the largest proportion of middle-class voters, was the most male, and was distributed evenly among the different age groups.

More-recent analyses of the Freedom Party's vote show that the percentage of workers voting for the party has increased dramatically. In the

1996 European election, 50% of blue-collar workers voted for the FPÖ, while only 25% voted for the SPÖ. Sully (1997) compares this with only 3% of workers voting for the FPÖ in 1983.

In the French case, Marcus (1995) notes that National Front's electorate was more working class than the mainstream right's electorate and also was more youthful and male. Géraud Durand (1996) describes how the electorate of the National Front went from being made up of older voters and the "bourgeoisie" from 1984 to 1988 to being a party that was able to get large percentages of young (18–25 years old), working-class, and unemployed voters in 1995–1996. Nonna Mayer (2002) also finds that the electorate of the FN tends to be less educated, anti-immigrant, male, and blue-collar through the 1997 election. Her more in-depth analysis of the 2002 elections indicates that these trends continued, but that Le Pen's electorate had grown and become more diversified. He had particularly increased his vote in rural areas and among farmers (Mayer 2002, 350). Mayer's data indicate that Le Pen is getting a greater percentage of older voters, and that those who voted for him in 1988 have continued to do so as they age (Mayer 2002, 349).

Jürgen Falter (1994) describes the German *Republikaner* and DVU (German People's Union) as *Männerparteien,* or men's parties. He also finds that they attract the young and those workers with little education who feel that their jobs are threatened. They do poorly among those who attend church regularly and those with a higher education. In their analysis of the *Republikaner* in Germany, Veen et al. find that *Republikaner* supporters tend to be farmers, self-employed, or members of the working class (Veen et al. 1993, 39).

Each of these authors describes the radical right attracting similar types of voters. In France and Austria the radical right has attracted a higher percentage of the vote and may be attracting voters beyond the basic core constituency of young, less-educated males. To compare the different types of radical right voters, I have combined data from surveys described in various studies; the results are shown in Tables 3.6 through 3.9.

The Radical Right Gender Gap

Nearly every study of the radical right has shown that men are more likely to vote for the radical right than women and that this gender gap has continued over time. Table 3.6 displays the percentage of men and women who voted for the radical right in national elections. Prior to Haider's 1986 takeover of the Freedom Party in Austria, the FPÖ had a

TABLE 3.6. *Gender Basis of Radical Right Vote (percentage)*

Year		Austria FPÖ	France FN	Germany REP
1988	Female		39	
	Male		61	
1989	Female		43	36
	Male		57	64
1990	Female	40		42
	Male	60		57
1991	Female			
	Male			
1992	Female		47	
	Male		53	
1993	Female	44	50	
	Male	56	50	
1994	Female		42	40
	Male		58	60*
1995	Female	38	40	
	Male	62	60	

* Estimate based on previous election data.
Sources: Betz 1994, 143; Perrineau 1997, 210; Plasser, Ulram, and Müller 1995, 150.

higher percentage of male than female voters (54% vs. 46%). This split was even starker in the 1995 legislative election. In this election, the Freedom Party's electorate was 62% male and 38% female. In the 1997 legislative elections in France the FN electorate was 60% male and only 40% female. The potential *Republikaner* electorate in Germany in 1998 was 52% male and 48% female, according to a survey by the Konrad Adenauer Foundation (Neu 1998).

In Germany, as in France and Austria, the vote for the radical right is predominantly male. Even in Austria, where the Freedom Party has achieved more than 25% of the vote, men are still more likely to vote for this party than women. The explanations for this gender gap are numerous. Most authors argue that the radical right's nostalgia for the past is not attractive to women voters. Pascal Perrineau notes that the increase in women's participation in the workforce and the fight for equality has led to insecurity in men. He argues that changes in the way politicians deal with nationalism have led some male voters to search for a "father figure," supplied by the National Front in the form of the party leader, Le Pen (Perrineau 1998). Betz argues that women are more involved in

TABLE 3.7. *Age and the Radical Right Vote*

National Front (1993)		*Republikaner* (1992)(1993)		Freedom Party (1994)(1993)	
Age	Percentage	Age	Percentage	Age	Percentage
18–24	15	18–24	16	<30	25
25–34	14	25–34	13	30–44	22
35–49	11	35–44	11	45–59	22
50–64	13	45–59	12	≥60	22
65+	12	60+	7		

Source: Betz 1994, 147; Plasser, Ulram, and Müller 1995.

social activities, such as attending church, and this involvement leads them to vote for the radical right in lower numbers than men, who are less likely to attend church than women (Betz 1994, 145). Mayer (2002) has argued that it is the violent nature of the radical right that repels women. However, I have found (Givens 2004) that even less violent radical right parties like the FPÖ attract more men than women, despite the charismatic appeal of a leader like Haider.

The Generation Gap

Young people may be more likely to vote for the radical right because they are more likely to be unemployed or because they do not have the same partisan connections as their parents. Often voters for the radical right are those who have not voted before.

Table 3.7 displays the percentage of each age group that votes for the radical right. According to this survey data, the radical right age profile is not necessarily as strongly oriented toward young voters as many authors indicate. One thing this table does not indicate is that the percentage of young radical right voters is higher than the percentage of young voters for the other mainstream parties. Instead, these data indicate that the vote for the radical right is spread out fairly evenly among the different age groups, with only a few percentage points of difference. The comparison of time periods I use in my analysis in Section 3.4 will indicate if this pattern has changed at all.

Class and Education

The survey data in Table 3.8 show that the radical right gets a higher percentage of blue-collar workers than of white-collar workers. This trend

TABLE 3.8. *Class Structure of the Radical Right Vote (percentage)*

	Austria (1995)	France (1993)	Germany (1990)
Blue-Collar	34	18	3
White-Collar, Government	20	12	1.1
Self-Employed, Farmers	na	15	1.3

Sources: Betz 1994, 156, 163; Plasser, Ulram, and Sommer 1996.

TABLE 3.9. *Education and the Radical Right Vote (percentage)*

	Austria (1994)	France (1993)	Germany (1990) by Age and Education	
Low				
(high school or less)	21	12	18–29	4.7
			30–39	3.3
			40–49	1.7
			50–59	2.0
			60+	1.4
Middle				
(technical school,	26	16	18–29	1.7
vocational school)			30–39	1.4
			40–49	0.6
			50–59	0.3
			60+	0.6
High				
(university or higher)	19	10	18–29	1.1
			30–39	0.3
			40–49	0.4
			50–59	0.0
			60+	0.7

Sources: Betz 1994, 156, 163; Plasser, Ulram, and Müller 1995.

has been well documented by Betz. In the case of the National Front, the percentage of workers increased from 18% in 1993 to 24% in the 1997 legislative election. Even in Germany, the percentage of blue-collar workers voting for the *Republikaner* is higher than the percentage of other types of workers. The percentage of blue-collar voters is the area of greatest similarity among the three radical right parties.

Education level is where the greatest difference appears among the countries. Table 3.9 indicates that the radical right parties in France and Austria actually get a higher percentage of middle-level voters, while the

German parties have a higher percentage of low-level voters. This difference indicates that radical right voters are not necessarily those with a low level of education. More careful analysis over time should be done to determine if the radical right is gaining among voters with higher levels of education. As noted earlier, the Freedom Party has traditionally drawn a portion of its voters from the more highly educated segment of society, but in more recent elections they also appear to be drawing more voters from the segment with less education.

Ecological Inference

Survey results for the German case are problematic because there are very few radical right voters in a sample. Where possible I have estimated the percentage of voters in particular social groups who have voted for the radical right. To estimate individual-level behavior I use Gary King's method of ecological inference. Ecological inference is a method used to infer individual-level relationships when individual-level data are not available. I have conducted an analysis of the German vote with data from the German 1990 *Bundestag* election. I am drawing on data from West Germany, which had 248 electoral districts.

The estimates are made using the software program King has designed. King's method estimates parameters based on a two-by-two table (Table 3.10). The table lists the two categories of interest on the vertical axis (e.g., blue-collar voters and all other voters) and the vote for two parties on the horizontal axis (in this case, the vote for the radical right, and the vote for all other parties). The known values are T, in this case the percentage of the vote received by the radical right; X, in this case the percentage of blue-collar workers in the voting population; and N, the number of eligible voters. This model gives estimates for ßb (percentage of category voting for RR) and ßw (percentage of category voting for other parties) based on a distribution of values, bounded by the highest and lowest possible values for each parameter.

I have collected data for the combined vote of the National Democratic Party (NPD) and the *Republikaner* (the radical right vote). Not all categories can be reliably estimated with this method. There are two aggregate categories I have estimated: youth (age 18–25) and blue-collar workers. The youth vote estimate indicates that 7.7% of voters between the ages of 18 and 25 vote for the radical right in Germany versus 2% of the rest of the population. Blue-collar workers also vote disproportionately for the radical right. The results indicate that 4.7% of blue-collar workers voted for the radical right versus 1% of all other types of workers. These results

TABLE 3.10. *Estimates for Ecological Inference*

	Model		
	RR Party Vote	**Other Party Vote**	**Population**
Category 1	ßb	1-ßb	X
Category 2	ßw	1-ßw	1-X
	T	1-T	
	Blue-Collar Vote		
	RR/Vote	**Other Party Vote**	
Blue-Collar	0.047	0.4	
Other	0.008	0.6	
	0.027		
	Youth Vote (18–25)		
	RR/Vote	**Other Party Vote**	
Youth	0.077	0.12	
Other	0.021	0.88	
	0.027		

Estimates are underlined.
X = Population of Category 1.
1-X = Population of Category 2.
Category 1 = Blue-Collar and Youth.
Category 2 = Other.
T = Total radical right vote.
1-T = Total other party vote.
Source: King, Gary. *EzI: An (Easy) Program for Ecological Interface,* 1997 Version.

support the survey data that show that the radical right in Germany is drawing a disproportionate percentage of its vote from young, blue-collar workers.

The data described in this section support my argument that the radical right electorates are very similar. To determine if traditional cleavages have less influence in the 1990s than in the 1980s it will be necessary to compare survey data from different time periods. I also look for evidence that the radical right parties' electorates are converging.

3.4. COMPARING ELECTORATES ACROSS TIME

The goal of this section is to determine if there is evidence that the electorates of radical right parties are converging. We have already seen evidence in the previous section that the traditional cleavages appear to have a stronger influence in Germany than in France or Austria. As with the mainstream parties, I focus mainly on the class composition of the radical right electorates, with a brief discussion of other categories.

I compare the composition of the radical right parties' voters to determine if the type of voter they are attracting in the mid-1990s is similar to that of the mid-1980s. I have chosen these time periods because they present the time when the radical right first had electoral success and a time when they had become established parties. The survey data are presented in Table 3.11. Since the results are from national-level surveys, the categories are not exactly the same for each country. Note that the data presented in the tables are the percentage of a particular social group that has voted for a party.

As noted, the radical right tends to attract a higher percentage of male versus female voters. This trend continues from the 1980s to the 1990s. As shown in Table 3.11, the radical right in each country has continued to attract nearly twice as many men as women.

In the area of education, both the *Republikaner* and the FN have continued their trend in attracting less educated voters. It is interesting to note that the FPÖ had its biggest increases in voters with a primary or secondary education. This could indicate that the traditional cleavage that the FPÖ represents is weakening, and that it is beginning to represent the less educated, who are more threatened by globalization.

In the age category, the trend also is toward an increase in the percentage of young voters attracted to each party. The main change from the 1980s is an overall increase in each category as the parties' percentage of the vote increased. However, the continuation of a higher percentage of young voters (under age 30) voting for the radical right than older voters continues the trend of radical right parties attracting younger voters.

One of the most striking instances of constituent profiles becoming similar is in the area of professions. As Betz found, the representation of blue-collar workers in the radical right electorate has increased steadily since the 1980s. This is true not only in France and Germany but also in Austria. Each of the radical right parties has shown a significant increase in the percentage of self-employed and blue-collar workers it is attracting.

In the case of class, it would appear that the decline in the influence of traditional cleavages has allowed the radical right to gain support from groups that previously were loyal to the mainstream parties. It is difficult to say definitively that the traditional cleavages no longer play a role in the radical right vote, but radical right voter profiles have become more

TABLE 3.11. *Percentage of Social Group Voting for Radical Right Party, by Country*

	FPÖ			FN			NPD REP	
Austria	'86	'94	France	'86	'97	Germany	'87	'94
Gender			Gender			Gender		
Male	12	28	Male	5.2	12.0	Male	0.3	2.5
Female	7	17	Female	3.2	7.5	Female	0.1	1.0
Education			Education			Education		
Primary	6	21	Primary	4.3	10.4	Primary	0.5	2.7
Secondary	11	26	Secondary	6.5	12.9	Secondary	0.2	1.5
University or	11	19	Vocational or	5.3	—	University or	0	0.5
Higher		19	Technical			Higher		
			University	2.4	6.0			
Profession			Profession			Profession		
Farmers	5	15	Farmers	1.9	4.2	Farmers	0	3.6
Self-Employed	15	30	Self-Employed	7.1	9.0	Self-Employed	0.5	2.2
Managers,	9	14	Managers,	3.5	4.1	Managers,	0.2	0.6
Professionals			Professionals			Professionals		
White-Collar	13	22	White-Collar	3.9	6.8	White-Collar	0.1	1.2
Blue-Collar	10	29	Blue-Collar	4.8	8.0	Blue-Collar	0.3	3.6
Age			Age			Age		
<30	12	25	18–24	7.4	10.0	18–24	0.2	1.5
31–44	11	22	25–34	4.1	12.2	25–34	0.2	2.1
45–59	6	22	35–44	3.1	9.6	35–44	0.1	1.7
≥60	8	22	45–54	4.9	9.8	45–59	0.2	1.9
			55–64	3.5	9.5	60–69	0.2	1.6
			≥65	4.4	7.4	≥70	0.7	1.2
TOTAL VOTE	9.7	22.5	TOTAL VOTE	4.2	9.6	TOTAL VOTE	0.3	1.8
			N	122	194	N	23	173

Sources: Austria: Plasser, Ulram, and Müller 1995, 354, 356, and 358. France: SOFRES *Post-Electoral Survey,* May 1988, N = 3000; SOFRES, CEVIPOF *Post-Electoral Survey,* May 1997, N = 3000. Germany: Forschungsgruppe Wahlen 1995; *Politbarometer West [Germany], 1977–1995 Partial Accumulation,* 1987 data N = 10,000, 1994 data N = 10,000.

similar at the same time that traditional support for the mainstream parties has weakened, particularly in France and Austria.

The German case stands out as a situation where traditional cleavages may be suppressing the vote for the radical right, but it is hard to make this argument, since the *Republikaner* is attracting the same types of voters as in France and Austria. German voters may have other incentives for choosing the mainstream parties. I explore other explanations for the differences in the German case in later chapters, focusing on the role of political institutions.

The survey data used in this chapter would indicate that the vote for the radical right is not only similar, but that the types of voters for each party are converging. In France, Germany, and Austria, the radical right parties are attracting less-educated, young, male, blue-collar voters. It is difficult to determine if this trend will continue, particularly as the fortunes of the parties change. This trend is consistent with previous analyses of radical right voters. However, these data make it difficult to argue that the parties are attracting different types of voters, as Kitschelt has argued. When we stretch the time horizon of the analysis, we see that electorate differences become much less prominent across countries.

The hypothesis I set forth in Section 3.2 of this chapter indicates that traditional cleavage structures would affect a radical right party's constituency in the early stages of its development, but that influence would decline, leading to voter profiles becoming more similar across countries. The evidence presented earlier indicates that a change has occurred from the mid-1980s to the mid-1990s. The parties' constituencies have become more similar during this time, and the role of traditional cleavages does appear to be declining in general.

3.5. CONCLUSIONS

Even this analysis cannot get beyond the limitations of survey data, but the goal has been to use more-robust survey data and to compare different time periods to provide a more complete picture of the composition of the radical right vote. The survey and ecological inference data analyzed provide evidence that there is increasing similarity in the types of voters who support the radical right in France, Germany, and Austria.

Although I find some support for the hypothesis that traditional cleavages influence the radical right vote, cleavage structures cannot tell the whole story. For example, the consistent decline in the influence of cleavages cannot explain the difference in the vote for the radical right in Germany as compared with France and Austria. This analysis can provide only a partial explanation for the difference in the level of success of radical right parties.

The success of a radical right party, or any party, is not solely dependent on the strategy it pursues or the strength of traditional cleavages. Other factors play an important role in helping voters choose a party for which to vote. Who votes for a particular party also is dependent on voters' analysis of their environment. If they feel that they may be in danger of losing their job, or that there are too many immigrants where they live, they may be more likely to support a party that addresses those issues. Survey data are not adequate to answer these types of questions, so some authors have used aggregate economic and demographic data to determine if immigration or unemployment has an effect on the radical right vote. In the next chapter I turn to an aggregate data analysis to explore variations in the radical right vote.

4

Immigration, Unemployment, and the Vote for the Radical Right

4.1. INTRODUCTION

The rise of radical right (RR) parties in Western Europe has led to the politicization of issues such as immigration, making them more salient to voters. Do socioeconomic variables such as unemployment and immigration have direct influence on the vote for the radical right? Are mainstream parties losing ground to the radical right in regions with high levels of unemployment and immigrants? Popular perceptions exist of depressed, industrial towns and regions being "swamped" by immigrants and turning to the radical right out of desperation. The radical right has used the issues of immigration and unemployment in an attempt to challenge the mainstream parties and increase its vote share. In this chapter I use aggregate data to focus on the effect of immigration and unemployment on the vote for the radical right. I test the hypothesis that the radical right vote is related to the geographic concentration of immigrants, particularly in regions where unemployment is high. Although there may be a relationship between these variables, I argue that this relationship cannot provide a causal explanation for the differences in the success of radical right parties.

The leader of the French National Front (FN), Jean-Marie Le Pen, has consistently linked the number of immigrants in France to the number of unemployed. His plans to repatriate immigrants and give French citizens preference in the job market were designed to strike a chord with working-class French voters. Likewise in Austria, the Freedom Party (FPÖ)'s "Austria First" petition drive was an attempt to push the great coalition government to toughen immigration control. The Freedom Party's leader,

Jörg Haider, has connected the number of immigrants to the number of unemployed in Austria, and the party has called for a reduction in the number of immigrants in Austria until full employment of Austrians has been reached ("Bündnis für Arbeit," FPÖ 1997). The Berlin *Republikaner* (REP) also recommends the prevention of the flow and employment of foreigners to avoid unemployment of German workers (*Berliner Programm*, Republikaner 1995). Whether bound by international constraints (Soysal 1994), the wishes of business for cheap labor (Freeman 2001), or simply wishing to avoid politicizing the issue, mainstream parties have tended to avoid discussing immigration (Cornelius, Martin and Hollifield 1994). Yet many Europeans have ranked immigration as an important problem, giving ammunition to the radical right. Further, several surveys in the 1990s showed that a majority of European voters considered unemployment one of the most important problems facing their country, which the radical right has linked to immigration.

Some commentators assume that the vote for the radical right is driven by levels of unemployment and/or the percentage of immigrants in a particular region. Yet authors such as Nonna Mayer (1989) and Michael Lewis-Beck and Glen Mitchell (1993) come to different conclusions in their analyses of the role unemployment and immigration play in the success of radical right parties in Western Europe. Unemployment levels have risen in most Western European countries in the 1980s and 1990s, with highs reaching 12% at the national level in France and Germany. Despite discontinuing the importation of labor in the early 1970s, the number of non–European Union (EU) immigrants has continued to grow due to family reunifications, the demand for illegal labor, and refugee movements. Several authors (Ignazi 1992, Betz 1994, Kriesi 1995) point to these factors as putative causes of the increase in votes for radical right parties; however, the findings of authors[1] who have empirically tested the effect of unemployment and immigration on the radical right vote are contradictory.

It is clear that radical right parties have used the issues of immigration and economic uncertainty as part of their electoral campaigns. Voters who live in regions with high numbers of immigrants may feel that these immigrants are in competition with them for jobs. One would think that given the radical right's reliance on these issues, *there should be a positive relationship between unemployment, immigration, and the vote for the radical right.*

---

[1] Mayer 1989, Lewis-Beck and Mitchell 1993, Swank and Betz 1995, Jackman and Volpert 1996, Chapin 1997.

To examine this argument I test the following hypothesis:

HYPOTHESIS 1: Due to the similar positions of radical right parties on the relationship of unemployment to immigration, there will be a positive relationship between unemployment, immigration, and the vote for the radical right.

The null hypothesis is that these variables will have no impact on the vote for the radical right. Using a linear regression model, I test the relationship between the vote for the radical right, immigration, and unemployment. I expect the relationship of these variables to be similar in France, Germany, and Austria, since the radical right parties have pursued similar strategies in each country.

I also consider an alternative hypothesis. There may be a negative relationship between the percentage of foreigners in an area and the vote for the radical right. Those who have regular contact with immigrants may see them as less of a threat as misperceptions break down (Allport 1954). Immigrants may also "self-select" and choose to live in areas where natives are more open to the presence of foreigners.

To place the analysis in context, I compare the results for the radical right parties to the same regressions for the mainstream parties. Radical right parties do not exist in a vacuum. The vote for the mainstream parties also may be affected by unemployment and foreigners. The results for the mainstream parties can help to indicate if there is evidence of general economic voting and how the pattern of the vote for the radical right parties varies from that of the mainstream parties.

The social democratic parties in the countries I am analyzing are considered pro-labor and tend to support industries that might otherwise be in danger of failing. I would expect the rate of unemployment to be positively related to the vote for labor-oriented social democratic or communist parties. However, this does not mean that there will be a negative relationship between unemployment and the vote for the conservative parties. If the conservative party has mainly been in opposition, there also could be no relationship or even a positive relationship with unemployment, since an incumbent is more likely to be blamed for economic problems leading to increased unemployment.

The relationship between the mainstream party vote and the percentage of foreigners in a region is more complex. If there is a positive relationship between foreigners and the radical right vote, I would expect to see a positive or no relationship between foreigners and the vote for conservative parties and a negative relationship with the social democratic vote. Social democratic parties are seen as being "easier" on immigrants than conservative parties (Money 1995). Also, conservative parties tend to be in direct competition with the radical right, so they are more likely to respond to the radical right on the immigration issue.

The dependent variable in this analysis is electoral success of radical right parties as measured by the percentage of the vote received in parliamentary elections from the 1960s to 1994, using electoral returns at the *Land* (state) level for Germany and Austria. For France, I focus on legislative elections from 1973 to 1997 at the regional level since there was no significant radical right party until the 1970s.[2] The data for each region and year are pooled by country. The explanatory variables are unemployment and the number of foreigners in each region in the year of a legislative election.

Figure 4.1 displays the percentages of unemployment, foreigners, and the vote received by the radical right over time in each country at the national level. The percentage of foreigners has increased significantly in Austria and Germany despite a stop in the recruitment of labor in the 1970s. The percentage of foreigners also has increased in France, but it has appeared to level out since the 1970s.[3] The percentage of unemployed has increased quite dramatically in France and Germany. Unemployment also has increased in Austria, but it has not reached the same levels as in France and Germany.

A positive relationship between the vote for the radical right and the rate of unemployment or immigrants in a region does not necessarily indicate that the unemployed (or immigrants) are voting for the radical right. An "ecological fallacy" can occur when aggregate data are used to infer individual-level relationships. The point of this analysis is not to infer individual behavior. This analysis will simply test if the vote for the radical right is higher in regions where unemployment and immigration are high.

As we have seen, many previous studies on the radical right focus on voting behavior. These authors use survey data for their analyses. However, it is difficult to draw conclusions from cross-national surveys, since the number of radical right voters in a sample is usually very low. In order

---

[2] There are 10 *Länder* (states) in Germany (excluding Berlin and East Germany), 9 *Länder* in Austria, and 21 regions in France (data for Corsica was missing for several years). The German data covers 9 elections, the Austrian data 9 elections, and the French data 7 elections.

[3] The number of foreigners in the French case is understated due to the higher number of naturalizations as compared with Germany and Austria.

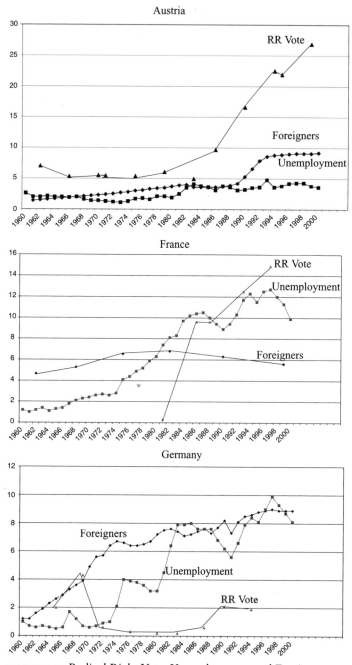

FIGURE 4.1. Radical Right Vote, Unemployment, and Foreigners

to avoid this problem, several authors look at the economic and political factors that may make the environment more or less conducive to
the success of radical right parties. These analyses tend to use aggregate
data at the national level in a large number of countries. In contrast, I
use aggregate data at the regional level in my three cases to determine
if socioeconomic variables play a role in the vote for the radical right.
This allows for a more specific and focused look at potential explanatory
factors. National-level analyses overlook the variance in the radical right
vote that occurs within countries. Most political parties have particular
regions in which they have historically performed better than others. For
example, in Austria the average vote for the FPÖ is only 5% in Burgenland
but reaches 16% in Carinthia.

Heino von Meyer and Philippe Muheim argue, "[E]ven in a globalising
economy, the labour market that directly affects most people and firms
remains regional or even local in scope" (von Meyer and Muheim 1996,
32). Labor markets tend to be larger than electoral districts, but a national-
level analysis cannot capture labor market differences. A regional-level
analysis is large enough to capture labor markets but small enough to
capture areas where particular parties may have stronger constituencies.
This approach also is useful because it is difficult to capture the impact of
unemployment and foreigners in a national-level analysis, where regional
concentrations of these two factors are obscured.

The main focus of the next section is a discussion of unemployment and
immigration, and their relationship to voting in Europe. In Section 4.3, I
describe previous work that has used immigration and unemployment to
explain the rise of the radical right in Western Europe and the empirical
evidence used to determine if a relationship exists between these variables
and the radical right vote. In Section 4.4, I describe the empirical evidence
I use to test my hypotheses and present the results of those tests. I conclude
by discussing the implications of my analysis.

4.2. UNEMPLOYMENT, IMMIGRATION, AND VOTING IN EUROPE

In this section I describe the development of immigration into France,
Germany, and Austria. I describe the way in which voters may find a
connection between unemployment and immigration, and how this may
lead to a vote for the radical right. I also describe how politicians from
mainstream parties have attempted to use the issues of unemployment
and immigration to attract voters.

Attitudes Toward Immigration and Radical Right Voters

Countries in Western Europe imported foreign labor during the 1960s to address labor shortages. This importation of labor was generally halted after the oil shock of 1972. Despite discontinuing the importation of labor in the early 1970s, the number of non-EU immigrants has continued to grow due to family reunifications and refugee movements, as well as the demand for cheap, illegal labor. Austria was a way station for immigrants heading for Germany and other Northern European countries during the 1960s. Austria began to rely more heavily on foreign workers during the early 1970s, but the number of foreign workers in the country did not increase after 1973, at least not until the number of refugees from Eastern Europe rose dramatically after 1989. None of these countries currently considers itself to be a "country of immigration." Not only do they no longer officially import labor; they have introduced measures to reduce the number of asylum seekers and refugees entering the country, and to make it more difficult for immigrants to bring in family members.

In interviews with mainstream and radical right party legislators and party strategists in France, Germany, and Austria, unemployment was described as one of the most important problems facing each country. In France, interviewees felt that the combination of high unemployment and large numbers of immigrants in particular areas of the country had led to the increase in support for the National Front. One legislator noted that immigration would not be an issue if unemployment were not so high. The issue of unemployment has played an important role in party strategy in recent legislative election campaigns.

Why should unemployment or the percentage of foreigners matter in the vote for the radical right? Increases in unemployment mean a decline in living standards for those workers directly affected and also are a sign of adverse economic conditions. Lewis-Beck (1988) looks at the role of economics in elections in Western Europe and the United States. He argues that the impact of economic voting is stronger in some countries than others. For example, he finds that the impact of economic voting is stronger in Germany than in France. Despite these cross-national differences, he finds that "evaluations of collective economic performance and policy move the voter. In particular, in each of these nations retrospective and prospective evaluations of government economic management significantly influenced incumbent support" (Lewis-Beck 1988, 156). Several other studies such as those of Gerald Kramer (1971), D. Roderick Kiewiet (1983), and

Gregory Markus (1988) also find a relationship between national economic performance and the vote for incumbents. However, this relationship only helps to explain why an incumbent's support might increase or decrease. It does not help to explain why voters might turn to a radical right party.

The presence of foreigners is another factor that may lead to an increased vote for the radical right. The radical right's xenophobic stance has an added appeal for those who feel that cultural homogeneity is being attacked, or that foreign workers threaten their jobs or wage levels. Although there may be no direct connection between unemployment and immigrants, voters may perceive that a relationship exists, particularly when certain industries such as construction tend to employ large numbers of immigrants during periods of high unemployment.

Radical right parties are not the only parties to link unemployment to foreigners. As Susan Milner and René Mouriaux point out, "Jacques Chirac, as Prime Minister in 1975, publicly declared that with one million unemployed and one million immigrants, France had the answer to its unemployment problem staring it in the face" (Milner and Mouriaux 1997, 53). The communists in France also attempted to use the issue of immigration in the 1981 presidential election. A communist politician actually drove a bulldozer into a dormitory for immigrant workers. In Germany, Michael Minkenberg notes that "[i]n his first speech after being elected chancellor, Helmut Kohl declared *Ausländerpolitik*, or the policy dealing with foreigners, as one of the four pillars of his government" (Minkenberg 1998, 28). When Austria's Chancellor Klima (Social Democrats [SPÖ]) came to power in 1997, he chose Karl Schlögl as his minister of the interior. Schlögl took a hard stance on the entry of foreign workers and was criticized by some members of the party for following policies similar to those proposed by FPÖ leader Jörg Haider.

Despite occasionally being the first to raise the issue of immigration or connect it to unemployment, the mainstream parties have generally been unable to profit from their stance on these issues. Political parties have had a difficult time finding solutions for unemployment in Europe. Structural change, including constraints imposed by European monetary unification, has limited governments' ability to influence labor markets. The radical right's position as an opposition party makes it easier to be critical of the mainstream parties and capitalize on increases in unemployment rates, connecting them to immigration.

4.3. SOCIOECONOMIC VARIABLES AND THE RADICAL RIGHT

Many authors have attempted to explain the conditions that can account for the rise of the radical right and to identify who votes for these parties. Some authors (Kitschelt 1995, Betz 1991, Swank and Betz 1995, Jackman and Volpert 1996, and Kriesi 1995) analyze the radical right in several countries (including Austria, France, and Germany) and attempt to find broad explanations for the rise of the radical right, while other authors (Minkenberg 1992, Veen, et al. 1993, Mayer and Perrineau 1992) focus on single countries. As described in the previous chapter, the cross-national analyses tend to focus on who is voting for the radical right and to use survey data such as the *World Values Survey* and the *Eurobarometer* surveys to describe voters for the radical right. A few authors have begun to use aggregate data, to avoid the difficulties found in using survey data. Jackman and Volpert look at parliamentary elections in 16 Western European countries from 1970 to 1990. Swank and Betz compare the same 16 countries from 1981 to 1992. Both sets of authors analyze aggregate demographic and economic data at the national level.

I examine next two issue areas that most authors have used in their explanation of the increase in the popularity of populist, anti-immigrant parties:

1. *Economic crisis, including high unemployment,* has led to discontent with the mainstream parties and has created a pool of disgruntled voters, who then may vote for the radical right.
2. *High numbers of immigrants,* particularly from outside Western Europe, are seen as a threat to job security and cultural homogeneity, and the mainstream parties are not perceived as doing enough to control immigration.

These two issue areas are interrelated. Economic problems or economic uncertainty can lead to the use of immigrants as political scapegoats. The first issue focuses on the voter for the radical right as a protest voter. He or she may be employed, but the fear of unemployment leads to a protest of government policy. The second issue relates to xenophobia and economics (i.e., too many immigrants and not enough jobs) that may push a person to vote for a radical option and not the mainstream opposition. Several authors also look at these two factors in combination with other socioeconomic variables, so there may be a combined effect.

Issue Area 1: Unemployment and Economic Crisis

Why should unemployment matter to the success of the radical right? Unemployment can create a pool of disgruntled workers who may choose to vote for the radical right. Also, unemployment in general may create an environment that is conducive to the radical right by creating uncertainty for those whose jobs may be threatened or by providing an alternative to those who blame the mainstream parties for economic downturns. If unemployment is a factor in the radical right vote, then there should be a strong positive relationship between increases in unemployment and the vote for the radical right.

Jackman and Volpert (1996) use aggregate data at the national level to test several hypotheses, including the effect of unemployment on the vote for the radical right from 1970 to 1990. As noted earlier, the data are for 16 Western European countries. Jackman and Volpert's analysis also includes an institutional element, with variables for electoral disproportionality and the effective number of parliamentary parties. Using Tobit regression analysis, they find that "support for the extreme right is a function of the electoral threshold, the effective number of parties, and the rate of unemployment" (Jackman and Volpert 1996, 508). They point out that this positive relationship with unemployment is not necessarily an indicator that the unemployed are voting for the radical right in higher numbers, but that increasing unemployment provides a fertile environment in general for radical right appeals. The explanatory importance of *electoral* variables in their study is an important theme that my analysis develops and expand on in the chapters to follow.

Swank and Betz's regression analysis includes 32 different independent variables. For unemployment, they "find a positive, statistically significant effect of changes in youth unemployment rates on electoral support for [radical right] parties" (Swank and Betz 1995, 21). Unlike Jackman and Volpert, Swank and Betz do not find a significant effect of general unemployment. These two studies show that unemployment is a factor in the rise of the radical right, but it is not clear if this is because of youth unemployment or general unemployment. For my own model, I test the effect of general unemployment, since data for youth unemployment are not available at the regional level for each country. Youth unemployment is likely to be highly correlated with general unemployment.

In their study of the 1986 legislative election, Lewis-Beck and Mitchell (1993) use data at the department level to test the relationship between the vote for the National Front, crime, and the interaction between unemployment and immigration. They find a small correlation between unemployment and the National Front vote and argue that rather than simply responding to unemployment, voters for the National Front may see a connection between immigration and unemployment. They infer from their model that "[c]onstituencies with high crime rates, and a pronounced immigrant presence in the midst of elevated unemployment, are fertile ground for National Front recruiters" (Lewis-Beck and Mitchell 1993, 124).

Each of the studies described finds a positive relationship between unemployment and the vote for the radical right. My analysis explores the effect of unemployment at the regional level as well as the additive effect of unemployment and immigration on the vote for the radical right. I also add to previous analyses by systematically comparing the relationship across my three cases.

Issue Area 2: Immigrants

Although anti-immigrant rhetoric is a recurring theme for the radical right, it is not clear that the actual number of immigrants in a country has an effect on the success of the radical right. The findings in this area tend to be contradictory. If immigrants are a factor, there should be some relationship between the increase in the number of immigrants or foreign workers and the vote for the radical right.

Two of Swank and Betz's variables test the role of immigration and asylum seekers. They find that "the inflow of asylum seekers is significantly associated with support for [radical right] parties" (Swank and Betz 1995, 22). However, they find that their variable for net immigration does not have a significant effect on radical right support. Perhaps the combined effect of asylum seekers and immigrants (both counted as foreigners in statistical data) would be shown to have an effect on radical right support, but Swank and Betz do not test this directly.

Immigration pressure is not necessarily a factor in the success of the radical right. Kriesi argues that "[i]f the immigration pressure in a situation of economic crisis provides the general *catalyst* for the mobilization of the movements of the extreme right, it does not translate directly into a greater mobilization capacity of these movements" (Kriesi 1995, 26). He points out that of the countries he compares – France, Germany, Switzerland, and the Netherlands – France has the least immigration pressure and the strongest mobilization of the radical right (Kriesi 1995, 26). Thus, immigration may have an effect as an issue, but the actual numbers of immigrants in a country may not matter for the success of the radical right.

Mayer (1989) conducted an analysis of the vote for the National Front in Paris to determine if there was an "immigrant effect" on the vote. Based on her analysis of the *quartiers* (districts) in Paris, she finds no relationship between the number of immigrants, or the origin of the immigrants, and the vote for Le Pen and the National Front. Instead, she finds that the profile of the voters for the FN tends to be inconsistent and concludes that this perhaps indicates that the vote for the FN is more of a protest vote against the main parties rather than a sign of support for Le Pen's views on immigration. One problem with Mayer's analysis is that it focuses only on the region of Paris. The vote for the National Front in the Parisian region is not necessarily representative of France as a whole, since the National Front's main base of support is in the south of France.

Nonna Mayer has published the results of a broader analysis conducted of the FN during the 1997 and 2002 presidential and legislative elections. In her book (Mayer 2002), Mayer finds that the electorate of the FN is made up of two different groups. The first group comprises typical radical right voters (young, male, workers), and the second group is made up of those who are simply voting against the left and right mainstream parties. Mayer finds that immigration and unemployment play a very important role for FN voters, but that is not the only reason they vote for Le Pen. She also finds that the personality of the candidate plays an important role in the voter's choice. Mayer is mainly looking at survey data (rather than electoral data) and party positions on these issues, so it is not clear to what extent these different factors play a direct role in the FN vote.

Pierre Martin (1996) uses electoral geography to determine if there is a relationship between the location of immigrants and the vote for the FN. He finds that the success of the FN results from four factors: an economic situation marked by insecurity and unemployment, the presence of an immigrant population that is treated as a scapegoat, an ideological heritage after 1945 that did not delegitimize the use of scapegoats (with racist connotations), and a political situation that was open to the reactivation of this discourse (Martin 1996, 46). Martin's analysis indicates that high levels of unemployment and immigration exist in the areas where the FN has been successful.

The results of the analyses described are mixed. Some authors conclude that the actual presence of immigrants does not play a role in the success of the radical right. This seems counterintuitive, since the radical right attempts to tap into anti-immigrant sentiment. Lewis-Beck and Mitchell do find a positive relationship between foreigners and the radical right vote in France. My analysis tests the relationship of these variables in France and compares the results with those in Germany and Austria.

4.4. DATA ANALYSIS

I have collected data at the *Land* (state) level for parliamentary elections from the 1960s through 1998 for a total of 10 elections in Germany and elections from the 1960s through 1999 for a total of 10 elections in Austria. The data for France is at the regional level from 1973 to 1997 for a total of 7 elections. The data for each country are pooled, with the elections treated as panel data for the purposes of the time-series analysis.

France has a two-vote majority system, and the results used in this analysis are from the first round of voting. The German electoral rules are fairly complicated, but basically each voter has two votes. The first vote is for a specific candidate in the electoral district; the second is for a party with lists determined at the Land level. I use the results from the second vote, since a party's electoral strength is based on the second vote, making Germany the equivalent of a proportional representation (PR) system. Austria uses a proportional representation system with lists determined at the Land level. Although I won't be able to control for the difference in electoral rules, the electoral data are drawn from the stage of the electoral process where the radical right is most likely to receive votes.

To determine if a relationship exists between the vote for the radical right, immigration, and unemployment, I turn next to regression analysis. The model is represented by the equation:[4]

$$RRVote = \alpha + \beta_1(FOREIGN) + \beta_2(UNEMPLOY) + e$$

FOREIGN $=$ the percentage of foreigners in the population

UNEMPLOY $=$ the percentage of workers unemployed[5]

The coefficients are estimated using a form of ordinary least squares (OLS) estimates with panel-corrected standard errors.[6]

The estimates for the radical right are presented in Table 4.1. I have run separate regressions for each country, so that I can compare the results

---

[4] α is the equation intercept or constant, and e is an error term.

[5] The measurement of unemployment can only be considered consistent within each country, since countries use different methods to calculate unemployment.

[6] Based on the work by Beck and Katz (1995).

TABLE 4.1. *Regression Estimates by Country – Radical Right (panel-corrected standard errors)*

Country	Constant	Foreigners	Unemployment	R^2
Austria	−0.01	0.79**	2.40**	0.58
N = 90	(0.01)	(0.18)	(0.48)	
France	−0.08**	0.66**	1.35**	0.67
N = 147	(0.02)	(0.21)	(0.23)	
Germany	0.02**	0.02	−0.11	0.07
N = 100	(0.01)	(0.05)	(0.09)	

** Significant at the .05 confidence level.

by country. The results show that the coefficients for each variable are significantly different from zero in France and Austria, and neither variable reaches significance in Germany.

The results for Austria indicate that a 1% increase in the unemployment rate is associated with a 2.40% increase in the radical right vote (holding foreigners constant). The model predicts a 0.79% increase in the radical right vote with each 1% increase in the percentage of foreigners (holding unemployment constant).

To understand the substantive meaning of each regression it is useful to look at an example of the predicted value of the radical right vote for specific levels of the independent variables. For example, using the average values for Burgenland, the percentage of foreigners is 1.4% and unemployment is 3.6%. Model 1 for Austria predicts a radical right vote of 8.7% (assuming the value of the constant is zero).

Austria model 1:

$$\text{Predicted RRVOTE} = 0.79(\text{FOREIGN}) + 2.40(\text{UNEMPLOY})$$
$$0.79(1.4\%) + 2.40(3.6\%) = 8.7\%$$

The actual value for Burgenland is 5.4%.

The results for France also indicate a positive relationship between the independent variables and the radical right vote. The coefficients for unemployment and foreigners are both significant. However, in the German case, neither coefficient is significant, indicating that the percentage of foreigners and unemployment has no impact on the radical right vote in Germany. The results for France and Austria support the standard hypothesis that the radical right has received more votes in regions where unemployment and immigration are high. The German case does not support this hypothesis.

TABLE 4.2. *Regression Estimates by Country – Social Democratic and Communist Parties*

Country	Constant	Foreigners	Unemployment	R^2
Austria	0.49** (0.02)	−1.43** (0.19)	0.14 (0.51)	0.34
France, Socialists	0.24** (0.06)	−0.33* (0.15)	0.57 (0.63)	0.09
France, Communists	0.20** (0.02)	0.11 (0.13)	−0.91** (0.24)	0.25
Germany	0.44** (0.02)	−0.40** (0.18)	0.22 (0.25)	0.04

* Significant at the .10 confidence level.
** Significant at the .05 confidence level.

TABLE 4.3. *Regression Estimates by Country – Conservative and Liberal Parties*

Country	Constant	Foreigners	Unemployment	R^2
Austria ÖVP	0.54** (0.02)	−0.14 (0.15)	−3.78** (0.43)	0.55
France RPR/UDF	0.49** (0.04)	−0.49** (0.11)	−0.73 (0.47)	0.15
Germany CDU/CSU	0.47** (0.02)	−0.21 (0.17)	−0.68** (0.23)	0.19
Germany FDP	0.08** (0.01)	0.12* (0.07)	−0.18* (0.12)	0.08

* Significant at the .10 confidence level.
** Significant at the .05 confidence level.

I also expect to see a relationship between each of the independent variables and the vote for the mainstream parties, as described earlier. Therefore, I have run additional regressions for each of the mainstream parties. The results for the socialist parties are in Table 4.2, and the results for the conservative parties are in Table 4.3.

As discussed in the chapter introduction, for the socialist parties I expect to find a positive relationship between the vote and unemployment and a negative relationship between the vote and foreigners. For the conservative parties, I expect a negative relationship with unemployment and either a positive or no relationship with foreigners. Since the results for the radical right in Germany did not support the main hypothesis, I also would expect that the result for the mainstream parties in Germany might not support my hypotheses.

In Austria, the vote for the SPÖ has a significant negative relationship with the percentage of foreigners in a region. As the percentage of foreigners in a region increases, the vote for the SPÖ decreases. This is consistent with my hypothesis and indicates that voters may be responding to the immigration issue, seeing social democratic parties as "soft" on immigration. The SPÖ has been in government either alone or in coalition with the Austrian People's Party (ÖVP) or FPÖ since 1970. If the government is considered to have a poor record in controlling immigrants, the SPÖ should be losing ground in regions where there is a high percentage of foreigners.

The relationship between the vote for the SPÖ and unemployment is positive; however, it is not significantly different from zero. The SPÖ has not benefited from the increase in unemployment, probably because they have not been in opposition, which would allow them to avoid taking the blame for any increases in unemployment.

In France, the relationship of the socialist vote with foreigners is negative and significant at the .10 confidence level. The issue of immigration appears to have a similar effect on the socialist vote in France, as in Austria. There is also a positive but not significant relationship between unemployment and the vote for the socialists in France. Despite periods of being in opposition, the Socialist Party (PS) has not benefited from high unemployment levels.

For the communists in France, the relationship with foreigners is not significant. What is surprising is that the vote for the communists is significantly and negatively related to unemployment. The communists have actually performed better in regions where unemployment is low.

As in Austria, the vote for the Social Democrats in Germany is negatively related to the percentage of foreigners. Unemployment is not significant. Unlike the Austrian socialists, the German socialists were in opposition for many years during the time period analyzed. As with the radical right vote, the German case does not meet expectations. These socioeconomic factors do have some influence on the vote for the socialist parties, but the relationship is not as strong as that with the radical right vote.

The results for the conservative parties come closer to supporting my hypotheses. In Austria, the vote for the ÖVP has a significant negative relationship with unemployment, but it has no significant relationship with the percentage of foreigners. The ÖVP has apparently been hurt more by increasing unemployment than the SPÖ, although the ÖVP has not led the government since the 1970s.

The results for the French conservative parties indicate that there is a significant negative relationship between foreigners and the vote for the conservative parties. The results for France seem to reflect the fact that the conservatives have had little success in co-opting the issue of immigration from the FN. As would be expected in the German case, there is also a negative relationship between unemployment and the vote for the Christian Democratic Union/Christian Social Union (CDU/CSU). There is a significant positive relationship between foreigners, unemployment, and the vote for the Free Democrats (FDP), although this relationship may be due to the fact that the FDP was supportive of the new citizenship law that made it easier for non-German immigrants to gain citizenship. The FDP may be receiving higher percentages of the vote in regions that are more accepting of immigrants.

As expected for the conservative parties (with the exception of the FDP and foreigners), each case indicates a negative relationship between the party vote and each of the independent variables, although this relationship was not always significant. In general, the socialists were not doing any better in regions where unemployment was high, while the conservatives had a negative relationship with unemployment. It would appear that left and right parties are affected differently by "economic voting," with the conservative parties losing votes in regions of high unemployment. On the other hand, the socialists tend to get a lower percentage of the vote in regions where the number of foreigners is high. In these cases, it may be that the socialist parties are identified with policies that are "soft" on foreigners.

The regressions for the mainstream parties indicate that the relationship between these socioeconomic variables and the vote does fit a basic pattern, and they point to a possible relationship with the radical right vote. More explanatory work can be done in the cases where the results do not support the hypotheses. However, across countries the different parties are affected by these socioeconomic factors in similar ways.

4.5. CONCLUSION

In the chapter introduction, I hypothesized that there would be a positive relationship between immigrants, unemployment, and the vote for the radical right. The statistical analyses evaluated here provide evidence that the vote for the radical right in France and Austria is related to the presence of unemployment and foreigners. Clearly, there are differences in the extent to which these variables can help explain the radical right vote in the three countries included in this analysis. The direction of the relationship turns out to be similar for Austria and France but not for Germany.

The German case indicates that immigration is not playing a major role in the vote for the radical right, although it may be for the mainstream parties. The poor showing of the radical right in Germany must be explained using different causal variables.

What does this analysis tell us about the role of socioeconomic variables in the vote for the radical right? Socioeconomic variables do play a role in the radical right vote; however, the variables used in this analysis are not sufficient to explain differences in the level of success of the radical right. It is important to note that cause and effect are not clear. Radical right parties in France and Austria could be expending more resources in regions where unemployment and immigrants are considered a problem, or voters in these areas may be more responsive to the message of the radical right. In Germany, the radical right may not be pursuing an electoral strategy that would allow them to capitalize on unemployment or foreigners.

The interaction between party strategy and socioeconomic factors may play a role in the relationship of these variables to the radical right vote. The FPÖ's party leader, Jörg Haider, has been outspoken in his criticism of the government's immigration policy, and despite the fact that his electoral base is his home state of Carinthia, his party has performed well recently in regions such as Vienna, where there are large numbers of immigrants. In the case of Germany, the *Republikaner* and other radical right parties like the National Democratic Party (NPD) have attempted to create an electoral base in *Bayern* (Bavaria), but have been stymied by the success of the CSU, in part because the CSU is to the right of its coalition partner, the CDU, particularly on the issue of immigration. In the case of France, the National Front has performed well since its initial success in areas where there are high numbers of immigrants, particularly the area around Marseille. The regression results for France may be based simply on the party's strategy in terms of where they have built an electoral base, while in Austria the results may reflect the party's more recent success in areas where there are more immigrants.

The main implication of this analysis is that an environment where there are high numbers of immigrants and unemployed workers can be especially conducive to support for the radical right. This analysis cannot claim to predict individual-level behavior, but in the case of France and Austria, economic factors such as unemployment may play a role in increasing the insecurity of voters. The radical right parties tap into this insecurity and provide scapegoats in the form of immigrants. It is important to note, however, that the German case indicates that other factors, such as party strategy and electoral thresholds, also may play an important role in the vote for these parties. I theorize and test these crucial variables in the next chapters, attempting to go beyond previous institutional analyses by including coalition strategy and party factionalism as well as electoral variables.

APPENDIX

Notes on the Data

Where data were missing, linear interpolation was used to estimate the percentage of foreigners in a region.

In the French case, Corsica was not included in the analysis due to problems with data collection and comparability.

5

Coalitions and Strategic Voting

A Model

5.1. INTRODUCTION

Many attempts have been made to explain the success of radical right parties by looking at the relationship of the radical right vote with unemployment and immigration. In the previous chapter, a relationship was found between socioeconomic variables and the radical right vote in France and Austria, but this relationship does not provide a causal mechanism to explain the difference in the level of success of radical right parties. Having similar levels of immigrants and unemployment does not lead to the same relationship in Germany. In this chapter, I move beyond previous explanations for the success of radical right parties by focusing on the role of electoral systems and coalition strategies.

The electoral system in a country plays an important role in determining the ability of a small party to gain votes. Electoral systems often are designed to make it difficult for small parties to compete. This is usually done by the imposition of barriers such as electoral thresholds or requiring a certain number of signatures to be eligible for an election. Another way in which small parties are discouraged is coordination by the mainstream parties that leads to strategic voting. Strategic voting occurs when voters choose to vote for a party other than their preferred party because they are afraid of wasting their vote, or they are afraid that their least-favored party will win if they vote for their preferred party. *In electoral systems in which the mainstream parties can coordinate to encourage strategic voting, small parties will have difficulty attracting voters.*

This general hypothesis will be refined in the following chapter, to focus on the impact of strategic voting on the success levels of the radical right.

However, in order to develop the theory that will guide the analysis it is important to understand the basic features of electoral systems and the ways that mainstream parties coordinate, either to avoid competing with small, extreme parties or to use them as possible coalition partners.

Parties can coordinate in several ways, but the main focus of this chapter is on the combination of electoral rules (e.g., proportional representation [PR]) and parties' coalition signals prior to an election, which influences strategic voting. I also will examine the impact that factionalism has on the radical right's ability to coordinate with the mainstream parties. In general, the literature on electoral strategies has neglected the importance of coalition signals that parties make before an election. In some situations mainstream parties will signal their coalition preferences to *encourage* strategic voting, while in other situations they may signal coalition preferences to *discourage* strategic voting. The way that coalition signaling is used depends on the nature of the electoral system and the party system, which then determine voters' expectations.

The role of electoral systems has generally been neglected in studies of the radical right. In comparing radical right parties, authors such as Kitschelt (1995) and Betz (1994) do not systematically take the electoral system into account when considering the differences in the levels of success of these parties. Kitschelt does not consider variations in electoral systems to be an important factor in the success of radical right parties in Western Europe. He defends his stance on electoral systems by stating that "[w]hile electoral laws have a non negligible impact on party formation and the fragmentation of party systems taken by themselves, they explain very little about the actual dynamics of competition" (Kitschelt 1995, 60).

Several authors (Schlesinger and Schlesinger 1998, Sartori 1997, Fisichella 1984) discuss the negative effect of the French electoral system on the vote for extreme or anti-system parties. For example, Joseph Schlesinger and Mildred Schlesinger include an analysis of the *Front National* (FN) in their study of the effect of the electoral system on parties in France, noting that the FN has little chance of gaining seats in a system in which alliances are necessary to win seats. Authors often cite Germany's 5% electoral threshold as a hindrance to extreme parties in Germany, but the 4% hurdle in Austria has not had the same effect on the Freedom Party. In more recent work, Roger Eatwell (2000) and Cas Mudde (2000) do take the electoral system into consideration in their respective studies of the extreme right in Britain and the Netherlands. In the case of Britain, Eatwell argues that "the election system had several notable effects" on the extreme right (Eatwell 2000, 188). First, the electoral system makes it necessary to geographically concentrate votes in order to have any chance of winning a seat. Second, it causes factions in the mainstream parties to stick together rather than form new parties as they might in a proportional representation system. Third, it keeps the mainstream parties from forming alliances or deals with the extreme right. All of these factors have made it difficult for the extreme right to have any electoral success in Britain.

In the case of the Netherlands, Mudde (2000) finds it puzzling that the extreme right has had little success in a country with what he calls "extreme proportional representation" (Mudde 2000, 161). Voters don't feel they are wasting their vote since it only takes 0.67% of the vote to win a seat in the Dutch parliament. Mudde argues that the extreme right in the Netherlands has been poorly organized and has been unable to capitalize on nationalist sentiment, in a country where nationalism is fairly weak. He also notes that the extreme right has remained an outsider in the Dutch party system. The lack of cooperation with a more mainstream party may have had an impact on these parties. However, the success of Pim Fortuyn's party (List Pim Fortuyn) in 2002 indicates that it is possible for the radical right to have a breakthrough in the Netherlands. This also is a case where the mainstream parties cooperated with a more extreme party.

These studies of France, Britain, and the Netherlands each provide some evidence on the impact of strategic voting on the vote for the radical right. What is lacking is a guiding theory that would allow for comparative empirical analysis. In this chapter, I lay out the general theory behind strategic voting and develop the model that guides the empirical analysis in the following chapter.

5.2. STRATEGIC VOTING

One can argue that all voting is strategic, if one makes the assumption that voters are simply trying to maximize their utility. However, for the purposes of this book, strategic voting refers to very specific behavior on the part of voters. Strategic voting occurs when voters choose to vote for a party other than their preferred party because they are afraid of wasting their vote or they are afraid that their least-favored party will win if they vote for their most-preferred party. Not all voters will vote strategically, but a variety of studies have shown that parties that have no chance of winning a seat in an election will be strategically deserted (McKelvey and

Ordeshook 1972, Cox 1997, Alvarez and Nagler 2000, Blais et al. 2001). Several of these studies also have attempted to measure the prevalence of strategic voting, showing that the percentage varies anywhere from 3% in the 1997 Canadian election (Blais et al. 2001) to around 7% in the 1987 British general election (Alvarez and Nagler 2000). Although the actual number of strategic voters may be small, it can have a disproportionate impact on the outcome of an election.

A discussion of strategic voting usually begins with Duverger's Law (Duverger 1954). This law states that plurality rule electoral systems with single-member districts produce two-party systems. Voters in this type of system may not vote for a small-party candidate, since this would be a "wasted vote." In the years since Duverger explained his law, many authors have supported the argument that an electoral system influences voting and the number of parties in a system. For example, Sartori argues that "[e]lectoral systems have a two-fold effect: one on the voter, and one on the number of parties" (Sartori 1997, 32). He argues that majoritarian systems have a strong constraining effect on voters and that in pure PR systems voters are unconstrained. In a majoritarian system, voters are more likely to vote strategically for the top two parties, while in a PR system strategic voting is less likely, which results in a multi-party system.

Systems with PR, however, are not immune to strategic voting. Parties can induce strategic voting by presenting voters with a coalition option prior to an election. If voters know that their party has no chance of being part of a coalition, they may choose to vote strategically for another party that does have a chance. Evidence for this behavior has been developed in Gary Cox's (1997) work on strategic voting. He refines the theories developed by Duverger and expanded upon by Sartori. He demonstrates that electoral systems have an effect on voters and on party strategy – particularly in coalition formation. Cox emphasizes the role that strategic coordination by parties plays in strategic voting. He states that "the most important features of electoral systems are those that affect the making of electoral coalitions, whether explicit alliances negotiated between party leaders or tacit alliances worked out among voters through strategic voting" (Cox 1997, 67).

The basic model used by Cox is a coordination game, similar to the "battle of the sexes," in which a couple must agree on a rendezvous. They would prefer to spend the evening together, but they have different preferences about where they should spend the evening. But since both would prefer the other's choice of activity to spending the night alone, there is no dominant strategy. The two actors must then coordinate their rendezvous to avoid the worst possible outcome, which is arriving at different destinations.

Voters often face a similar dilemma when choosing between candidates (or parties). In an election with more than two candidates, if they choose their most preferred candidate when he or she has no chance of winning, their least preferred candidate may win. Therefore voters may choose to vote for a less attractive candidate, who nevertheless has a chance of winning.

Parties must decide the best strategy for attracting voters, given the potential for strategic voting. In the case of competition between the far right and mainstream parties, research has focused on the positions that parties take, particularly whether or not they take a harder line on immigration (Money 1995, Schain 2000) or if the radical right chooses the "winning strategy" (i.e., attracts a certain type of voter) in situations where the mainstream parties have converged (Kitschelt 1995). However, we must first understand a party's incentives to pursue a particular strategy, and this depends on whether the mainstream parties actually need to worry about competition from the radical right. This in turn depends on the structure of the party system, leading us to the key question: Can smaller parties compete with established parties in a particular system?

Electoral rules influence the number of parties in a system as well as party strategy and the coalitions they form. Cox analyzes the impact of strategic voting at the district level and shows that strategic voting imposes an upper bound on the number of viable candidates in a district, the $M + 1$ rule, meaning district magnitude (the number of candidates to be elected) plus one. However, Cox also argues that party strategy across electoral districts may distract voters from local considerations. Voters may look at national-level strategies in trying to determine the party (or parties) that has the best chance of forming a government (Cox 1997, 201–202). This can lead to voters deserting smaller parties if they don't have a chance of competing at the national level or being part of a coalition government.

Cox's theory provides the basis for understanding the role of coalitions and strategic voting in the success of radical right parties as well as their impact on the strategies of the mainstream right. The strategies of the parties and the responses of voters are influenced by the electoral rules under which the parties compete; electoral rules play an important role in voters' candidate or party choices and in determining party strategies. However, the key here is voter expectations. These expectations can be influenced not only by structural factors, such as district magnitude, but by the actions that parties take prior to an election.

5.3. STRATEGIC VOTING, COALITION SIGNALING, AND FACTIONALISM: THE MODEL

To compare different types of electoral systems, I use the following assumptions to guide my analysis of voter choice and party coordination.

1. Voters prefer to vote sincerely, but instrumental voters can be influenced by strategic considerations.
2. Voters make use of all available information about a probable electoral outcome prior to voting.
3. Parties understand voters' preferences and how the party's actions will influence instrumental voters.[1]

Although voters' true preferences are difficult to observe, assumption 1 emphasizes the fact that voters can choose to act strategically. For the purposes of this analysis, the term "instrumental voter" refers to those voters who focus on short-term outcomes and are not using their vote to show their allegiance for a particular cause (Cox 1997, 77). Specifically, the instrumental voters I focus on are those who would vote for the radical right, unless they have an incentive to vote strategically for another party. As Cox puts it, "Trailing candidates are deserted, not by all voters, but by all short-term instrumentally rational voters" (Cox 1997, 78). Assumption 2 simply requires that voters have access to and use the information that would lead them to vote strategically. Assumption 3 refers to coordination on the part of parties. Parties are active players in this model and will choose a particular course of action to induce (or not induce) strategic voting.

I examine three components of strategic voting: the electoral system, coalition strategy, and factionalization. Figure 5.1 displays the relationships between these variables, party strategy, and voter strategy. This figure is a basic model of the impact of party strategy on voter expectations that can then lead to strategic voting.

The electoral system provides incentives for strategic voting that also impact the number of parties in a system. Austria, France, and Germany are all multi-party systems. As multi-party systems, the parties often must coordinate to form coalition governments. The coalition structure in the three countries varies from the tendency toward great coalition in Austria, to the bipolar system in Germany, to the more fractured system in France, in which the coalition partners have varied over the years.

---

[1] These assumptions are similar to those in Bawn (1993, 967).

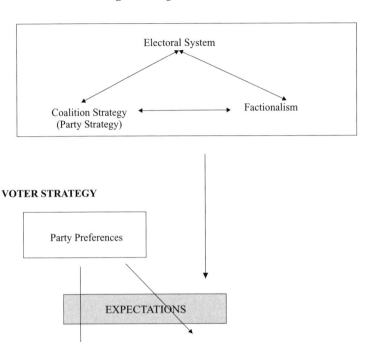

FIGURE 5.1. Voter Expectations and Party Vote

Specific types of electoral systems can influence voter expectations. PR systems tend to discourage strategic voting, but electoral thresholds as well as district magnitude can change the strategic calculus of a voter. High thresholds tend to encourage strategic voting. As noted earlier, the French system encourages the parties to form electoral coalitions, which also encourages strategic voting.

Coalition strategy has an impact on factionalism in the sense that it can push smaller parties to decide on a course of pragmatism, which will allow them to cooperate and possibly join in an alliance with more mainstream parties, or radicalism, in which the party stays outside of the party system, avoiding any moderation of its message. This divide between pragmatism and radicalism can lead to factionalism within a party, unless either the pragmatists or the radicals can maintain control. As factionalism increases, it can increase strategic voting if voters feel that their party is less likely to be able to form a coalition with a mainstream party. Factionalism can also lead to the formation of new parties, which can then lead to a split in the electorate of a small party, decreasing its ability to win seats or form a coalition, and increasing the likelihood that both parties will be strategically deserted. However, a party can become stronger if the split leads to ideological consolidation in one of the new parties.

It is important to note that the strategic interaction isn't only among voters; it also is between parties and voters. The voters are responding both to the incentives provided by the electoral system and the signals given by the parties. Coalition strategy is an important factor that parties can partially control in this model. They can decide if they want to signal to voters their coalition intentions prior to an election, thus encouraging them to vote strategically. When we incorporate voter strategy into the model for strategic voting (Figure 5.1) we can describe how the expectations created by the three components discussed earlier can influence vote choice. As Paul Thurner and Franz Pappi note,

Strategy comes in when probability beliefs are used in addition to preferences arising in electoral decisions... Voters seek to maximize their expected utility gain from the outcome of the election. This means that additional to utility considerations they have probability beliefs about how other voters will cast their ballots and which coalitions will be formed.   (Thurner and Pappi 1998, 3)

These "probability beliefs" are modeled as expectations in Figure 5.1. A voter begins with party preferences, is influenced by certain expectations of the electoral outcome, and chooses to vote for a particular party or coalition preference.

Coalition Signaling: The Battle of the Parties and Voters

Voters know that their single vote is not decisive in an election. Their votes must be aggregated to determine the final outcome. Therefore, Cox (1997) describes the basic idea of coordination as the classic "battle of the sexes." As Cox states, "The players in the game would prefer to

Pat

	Opera	Fight

		Opera	Fight
Chris	Opera	2,1	0,0
	Fight	0,0	1,2

FIGURE 5.2. The Battle of the Sexes. In this model, a couple ("Chris" and "Pat") differ about where to spend an evening.

coordinate their actions on some one of two (or more) possibilities but they disagree over which of these possibilities ought to be the one on which they coordinate" (Cox 1997, xiii). Figure 5.2 displays the basic model for this coordination game. There are two Nash equilibria[2] in this normal form game.

The game that parties and voters play is a bit more complex, since there are usually more than two options over which they must coordinate. However, when one includes coalition preferences, the number of options is decreased. If voters have certain expectations about the coalition government that will be formed, a radical right voter will either vote sincerely or strategically for another party as part of a coalition. If a vote is going to be close, and a vote for the radical right would hurt the chances of the preferred coalition, the instrumental radical right voter will vote strategically for his or her preferred coalition partner (e.g., a mainstream right party). However, if the radical right party is part of a coalition, or a vote for the radical right will have no impact on the outcome, the voter is more likely to vote sincerely.

The coordination game can be modeled as being between the voters who would prefer to see a particular type of coalition and the parties that would make up that coalition. The parties need to make sure that voters know that they are not wasting their vote when voting for the coalition partners. Voters need the appropriate information to make the right party vote.

The game begins with the calling of an election. The parties then decide whether they will signal their coalition intentions or not. It is important to note here that voters are more likely to pay attention to the coalition signals given by the mainstream parties, since these are more credible

---

[2] "[E]ach player's predicted strategy must be that player's best response to the predicted strategies of other players...no single player wants to deviate from his or her predicted strategy" (Gibbons 1992, 12).

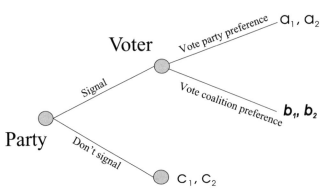

FIGURE 5.3. The Party and Voter Game

than those signals given by a small challenger party, so the focus here is on the signals being given by the mainstream parties. The voter then decides whether she or he will choose to vote sincerely or not. The game is displayed in Figure 5.3.

I assume that parties would prefer to not signal their coalition preferences in order to allow themselves room to maneuver after an election. From the assumptions described earlier, voters should prefer to vote sincerely. However, instrumental voters and parties will act strategically when necessary to achieve their preferred outcome. The possible outcomes for player 1 are a_1, b_1, and c_1. The possible outcomes for player 2 are a_2, b_2, and c_2.

Based on these assumptions, the preferences of the players would be ranked as follows:

Party: $b_1 > c_1 > a_1$
Voter: $a_2 > c_2 > b_2$

Using backward induction (Gibbons 1992, 58–61; Golden 1997, 29) we know that voters will never choose a_2 because we have assumed that they will choose to vote for a moderate coalition if their expectation is that the coalition they prefer may lose if they vote sincerely. Since this is a game of complete information, the party knows that the voter will choose to vote strategically if the party signals its coalition preferences. The only possible equilibrium is that in systems where strategic voting is more likely, parties will attempt to induce strategic voting by stating their coalition intentions, and voters will vote strategically (b_1, b_2).

The following chapter explores hypotheses based on this aspect of the model, as well as the other factors related to strategic voting in each of my cases. I begin in the next section by examining some of the more general questions and hypotheses related to this model.

5.4. QUESTIONS AND HYPOTHESES

If a voter prefers to vote for a far right party, why would she or he choose to vote strategically for another party? The basic idea is that instrumental voters will strategically abandon a party if they feel their vote will be wasted. Factors such as the electoral system and factionalism can have an impact on voters' expectation as to whether their vote will be wasted or not. However, we can move beyond this basic hypothesis and look specifically at the ways in which parties can attempt to influence voter expectations. Based on the model described earlier, voters who feel that their vote may be wasted may choose another party in order to vote for their preferred coalition outcome. This leads to my first general hypothesis:

H1: Instrumental voters are more likely to abandon their preferred party if they know it has no chance of being part of a coalition.

Parties play a strategic role in this model. They will attempt to induce a strategic choice on the part of instrumental voters in order to ensure that they receive the highest number of votes possible, particularly in systems that encourage strategic voting.

H2: A party will actively attempt to influence a voter's expectations of a coalition outcome when there is a challenger (e.g., radical right) party.

It is important to note that it is not always in a party's interest to signal to voters its coalition preferences. In systems where it is difficult to encourage strategic voting, a party may not want to signal its coalition preferences since its choice of a more extreme coalition partner might push away some of its more moderate voters.

H3: In systems that discourage strategic voting, parties may avoid signaling coalition preferences, if it will push more moderate voters to another party.

These three general hypotheses provide a basis for the country-specific hypotheses that are developed in the next chapter.

5.5. CONCLUSION

The study of strategic voting is a useful tool for examining the relative success of small parties. Established parties often have an incentive to try to shape voter expectations so that they can head off challenges by smaller or more extreme parties. Sometimes it will be advantageous to an established party to publicly refuse to ally with a challenger party, but this may not always be the case. The variations are likely to be systematic, and they can offer testable predictions for comparative analysis. The main purpose of this chapter has been to adapt theories of strategic voting to explain voter behavior and party strategy, particularly in relation to coalition signaling. Using a set of guiding assumptions, I developed a model that allows me to present a series of specific hypotheses for the cases that are analyzed in the next chapter.

6

Coalitions and Strategic Voting

Analysis

6.1. INTRODUCTION

In this chapter, I analyze the role of strategic voting and strategic coordination in the vote for the radical right in France, Germany, and Austria. As described in the previous chapter, voters have varying expectations that influence their decision to vote sincerely or strategically. Those expectations are influenced by the party system and the electoral system. The model that was developed in the previous chapter guides the hypotheses for each of the cases.

France's electoral system has developed into a bipolar party system, with moderate left and right parties alternating in government. Despite the bipolar nature of the French party system, the National Front (FN) managed to gain about 15% of the vote in the first round of the 1997 legislative election, mainly at the expense of the conservative parties. Germany's and Austria's proportional representation (PR) systems have created opposite outcomes, in terms of the success of the radical right. In Germany, the radical right has not been successful in getting above the 5% electoral threshold. In Austria, the Freedom Party (FPÖ) received 27% of the vote in the 1999 legislative election. The relative success of the radical right in France and Austria leaves no doubt that the FN and FPÖ have solid bases of support, but the FN won only one legislative seat in the 1997 election as compared with the 52 seats held by the FPÖ (out of 183). Survey data show that the radical right has similar levels of potential support in France, Germany, and Austria.[1] Why is the *Republikaner*

---

[1] See Chapter 1 for survey results.

(REP) receiving such a low percentage of the vote in Germany? Why isn't the National Front getting more than one seat in the French legislature?

The signals that parties send to voters in regard to coalition formation are important prior to and during elections. In France, parties often have used the first round of voting as a type of primary, to determine which party would represent the left or right in the second round. The success of the FN complicated matters for the mainstream right parties in France, since they could no longer count on making it into the second round. This led to the mainstream right parties agreeing (in most cases) on a single candidate prior to the first round of voting. In Germany, the Free Democrats (FDP) chose to continue their coalition with the Christian Democrats (CDU/CSU) in the 1998 election. In this election, the FDP was faced with the possibility of receiving less than 5% of the vote, according to pre-election surveys. The FDP had to pursue a strategy that would ensure that voters would choose to vote for the CDU/CSU–FDP coalition rather than "waste" votes on extreme parties.

In Austria, the great coalition made sending coalition signals irrelevant. Both the Social Democrats (SPÖ) and the Austrian People's Party (ÖVP) made threats that the other would form a government with the Freedom Party. However, voters' experience had mainly been with the great coalition, and, in many ways, the vote for the FPÖ was a vote against both of the great coalition parties.

The main argument in this chapter is that the success of radical right parties can be explained by their ability to compete in particular electoral systems. I argue that *the electoral system in Germany makes it more difficult for a radical right party to win votes, while the electoral system in France makes it more difficult to win seats.* In the case of Austria, *great coalition governments and the PR electoral system provide less incentive for strategic voting.* I support these arguments using the model developed in the previous chapter, in which instrumental voters base their vote choice on strategic considerations, influenced by the coalition signals made by the mainstream parties.

I begin this analysis by examining the electoral systems, factionalism, and coalition structures in Austria, France, and Germany. I also explain the specific hypotheses for each case that guide my analysis. What happened in the actual elections is described in Section 6.3, along with the data analysis that tests each of the hypotheses. The results of the analysis are summarized in the chapter conclusion.

6.2. ELECTORAL SYSTEMS, FACTIONALISM, AND COALITIONS

Figure 5.1 in Chapter 5 displayed the three factors that influence strategic voting: the electoral system, factionalism, and coalition signals (party strategy). Each of these factors influences the expectations of voters and can cause instrumental voters to vote strategically, rather than sincerely. In this section, I provide information on each of these factors for the three cases and then develop hypotheses specific to each case.

Austria – Electoral System

After World War II, Austria used a system of proportional representation, with 25 electoral districts and 165 legislative seats. From 1970 until 1992 Austria used a system of proportional representation with each of the 9 *Länder* (states) considered to be an electoral district. Seats in the legislature were increased to 183 and were first distributed at the *Land* (state) level, with the number of seats for each *Land* being based on the population. In the second round, the country was divided into two larger districts, and any unused votes from the first round went toward seats in the second round. In the second round, the seats were divided using the d'Hondt system that favors larger parties.[2]

In 1992, the Austrian government introduced a new electoral system that divided the 9 electoral districts into 43 regional electoral districts. A new first stage was added in which seats are distributed at the regional district level. After the first stage, seats are distributed at the *Land* level, then the national level. Parties must win one seat at the regional level or receive at least 4% of the votes at the national level to participate in the second and third stages of seat distribution (Müller 1996, 70). This system was first used in the 1994 legislative election.

In the election process, a voter chooses one party from a list. The first party that appears on a ballot is the strongest party from the previous election. A voter can also write in the name of a preferred candidate from the list of the party already chosen on the ballot. A candidate gets a point for each ballot with his or her name written in and can automatically qualify for a seat if the number of points received equals the number of votes needed to qualify for a seat. In the new electoral system, a candidate

---

[2] Chapter 2 of Lijphart (1994) goes into more detail on the different types of divisors for PR systems.

can win a seat at the regional level if he or she received half as many preference votes as required for a seat. However, it is rare for a candidate
to win a seat via preference votes. For example, in 1994, 15 candidates
received enough preference votes to win seats, but they all led their respective party lists and would have been elected in any case (Müller 1996, 71).
The parties have occasionally used preference votes as a way for voters to
indicate a preference for a chancellor candidate. The new law has helped
to personalize elections but has had little effect on voting at the national
level.

Factionalism

As described in Chapter 2, for most of its history, the Austrian Freedom
Party was divided into two camps, the liberal faction and the German-
nationalist faction. The liberal members of the party gained control of
the party during the 1970s, when the party began to show more sympathy for the Social Democrats, leading up to its coalition with the SPÖ in
1983. The party's decline in the polls during this coalition led to a struggle
between the liberal and the German-nationalist factions within the party.
This struggle ended soon after Jörg Haider's ascension as party leader
in 1986. The liberal faction soon broke away and created its own party,
the Liberal Forum. However, the split actually helped Haider consolidate his power within the party. The Liberal Forum was unable to compete with the Freedom Party and eventually went below the 4% threshold required for representation in the 1999 legislative election. In this
case, the Freedom Party became a stronger party once the liberal faction
had left.

Coalition Structure/Strategy

Austria's tradition of three *Lager* (camps) has had a strong influence on
the number of parties in the system. The three main parties in the system
correspond to the *Lager* that developed in Austrian society in the late
1800s: the socialist camp, represented by the SPÖ; the Catholic or Christian camp, represented by the ÖVP; and the German-nationalist camp,
represented by the FPÖ. The two main parties are the SPÖ and the ÖVP,
but the FPÖ also has had regular representation in the Austrian *Bundesrat*
(upper house).

With the change from 9 to 43 electoral districts, the average district
magnitude (number of candidates elected in a district) in Austria went

from 20.3 to 4.25. Despite this decline, district magnitude in Austria remains relatively high. This high district magnitude in Austria should encourage the proliferation of parties, but it is only in the last few elections that new parties like the Greens have made it into parliament. Until 1986, Austria had a bipolar or two and one-half party system, with the FPÖ making up the "one-half" party. Since 1986, the two main parties in Austria have been faced with the strategic dilemma of how to deal with the increasing success of the FPÖ.

An important factor in strategic coordination and voting in Austria is that the SPÖ and ÖVP formed a "great coalition" from 1945 to 1966 and again from 1986 to 1999. The two coalition partners developed the *proporz* system, in which the distribution of civil service (including nationalized industries) and cabinet posts was based on the result of the previous general election. Over time, the importance of party ties has diminished in the bureaucracy, but it has not completely disappeared. The *proporz* system has led to a great number of scandals and a growing disenchantment with the two main parties. The FPÖ was excluded from the *proporz* system, and it has used this exclusion to emphasize its role as a true opposition party.

The *proporz* system formalized coordination between the two main parties, and, even when they weren't in a coalition, the SPÖ and ÖVP cooperated on legislation. It has been difficult for either of the two main parties to act as opposition in this situation. This played an important role with voters when they became dissatisfied with the government during the 1990s. The FPÖ, as the outsider, could claim to be the only party of change.

The FPÖ took over the "third *Lager*," or German-nationalist camp of Austrian politics, and it therefore maintained continuity with Austria's traditional party system. The party has been contesting elections since the end of World War II and has developed a loyal base of support, although the composition of this base of support began to change in the 1990s, as shown in Chapter 3. Voters have little incentive to strategically desert the FPÖ, particularly now that there are even smaller parties that have gained seats in the legislature. The PR system ensures that the FPÖ will win seats. Voters don't have any reason to believe that the FPÖ will not win seats, despite the 4% threshold. The problem for the FPÖ, however, is that it needs a coalition with one of the other parties to get into government. The great coalition was the mainstream parties' way of coordinating to keep the FPÖ out of government, since they cannot keep them out of the legislature.

The great coalition is not the only option for the mainstream parties. In the late 1960s and early 1970s, each party was able to govern alone, either with a majority or as a minority government. Both parties would prefer this option to the great coalition; therefore they try to appeal to voters to gain a majority of seats. However, voters are aware of survey results that show that in more recent elections neither the SPÖ nor the ÖVP can win enough votes to claim a majority.

The mainstream parties have no electoral coalition strategy that can induce strategic voting. On top of this, the large size of the districts in Austria makes it difficult for voters to know which list will win the most seats in their district, or how this will affect the final outcome. As Cox notes, "the quality of voter information regarding candidate chances declines with district magnitude" (Cox 1997, 105). This makes it less likely that instrumental FPÖ voters will vote strategically for one of the top two parties. Although Cox notes that social cleavages (i.e., the *Lager*) have played an important role in maintaining Austria's two and one-half party system, a clear change occurred during the 1990s. More voters, particularly blue-collar workers, were willing to give up their traditional party ties to vote for a party that more clearly represented their perceived interests.

The factors described earlier make strategic voting less likely in Austria than in other countries with PR systems. Cox's theory would predict that strategic voting would occur when voters are unsure whether the first- or second-place party is going to win more seats. Despite this, since radical right voters in Austria knew that a great coalition was likely to form, and they knew that their party would win seats, they were less likely to vote strategically than radical right voters in different systems.

HYPOTHESIS 1: Even if an election is close, instrumental radical right voters will not vote strategically for one of the top two parties in a PR system with the following conditions: the outcome of a prior election was a great coalition government, and district magnitude is high.

In the case of Austria, the goal of the analysis is to determine if there is evidence of strategic voting. The discussion earlier has shown that high district magnitude and great coalitions tend to reduce the possibilities for strategic voting. This will be tested by determining if there is a relationship between the vote for the FPÖ in Austria and the absolute difference in the vote between the SPÖ and ÖVP. If strategic voting were occurring, I would expect the vote for the FPÖ to decrease as the competition between the SPÖ and ÖVP increased and the difference in the vote between the two parties decreased. Since strategic voting is unlikely in Austria, I expect to find no significant relationship between these variables.

France – Electoral System

France has a single-member dual-ballot system (SMDB), with the exception of the brief switch to PR in 1986. The current law states that a candidate who wins more than 50% of the votes cast in the first round is elected (i.e., a majority of votes wins the seat). If there is a runoff, anyone with 12.5% of the vote (based on the total voters registered in the district) may advance to the second round. The second round of the election is held one week after the first round. The candidate with the highest percentage of the vote in the second round wins the seat (i.e., a plurality of votes wins the seat).

The result of France's electoral system is a multi-party system, but a two-block system. Four mainstream parties have consistently contested elections in France since De Gaulle resigned as president. The liberal/conservative Union for French Democracy (UDF) and the conservative Gaullist Rally for the Republic (RPR) are the main right-conservative parties, and the Communists (PC) and the Socialists (PS) are the main left parties. The UDF and RPR dominated governing coalitions until the socialists made their electoral breakthrough and won the legislative election in 1981. Often, coalitions are made with other small parties, such as the Green Party on the left and the MDR (*Mouvement des Réformateurs* – Reform Movement) on the right. The National Front represents the extreme right of the party spectrum.

Factionalism

The FN has generally been under the firm control of Jean-Marie Le Pen since it was formed in the early 1970s. Le Pen was only willing to cooperate with the mainstream parties on his own terms. However, Bruno Mégret brought a new more pragmatic approach when he joined the party in 1987. Mégret was a member of the conservative Gaullist Rally for the Republic and joined the FN's party list during the 1986 election, in which the electoral rules were changed to proportional representation. Over time, Mégret became Le Pen's heir apparent, after being the director of Le Pen's presidential campaigns in 1988 and 1995 (DeClair 1999). However, Mégret's rise in influence also led to friction between the two men. Mégret did not approve of many of Le Pen's anti-Semitic and inflammatory statements, which did not sit well with Mégret's desire to have a rapprochement with the mainstream right. Further, unlike Le Pen, Mégret was formerly a mainstream French politician. In an interview conducted by the author, Mégret (1997) stated that he would continue to propose accords with the mainstream right parties. DeClair notes that,

> If the Front succeeds in negotiating future electoral alliances with the mainstream right, it will be thanks to Mégret, who is viewed as one of the most likely frontistes [*sic*] to craft such an agreement. Such a turn of events would not sit well with the party's hard-core nationalists, who are more interested in ideological purity than political expedience.   (DeClair 1999, 163)

DeClair's assessment (made in 1997) was prescient. A power struggle would develop between the forces of pragmatism, represented by Mégret, and the forces of purity, represented by Le Pen and many of his close advisors. DeClair notes in the afterword to his book that in December of 1998, a split began between Mégret and Le Pen that ended with the party breaking in two.

There was clear factionalism in the FN, particularly as to whether the FN should reach out to form electoral alliances with the mainstream right. These alliances did not occur, although this was not necessarily due to a lack of desire on the part of leaders in the FN. However, this lack of alliances clearly had an effect on the FN's ability to win seats in the National Assembly, as described in the next section.

Coalition Structure/Strategy

To win seats in the French Assembly, parties on the left and right (informally) form coalitions at the district level after the first round of the election, to present one left and one right candidate in the second round. Usually, the coalition candidate with the highest percentage of the vote in the first round advances to the second round as the representative of both parties. These agreements allow the right or left to get a high enough percentage of the vote to win a district.

Tsebelis (1990) finds that in the case of France, the need to form coalitions affects party strategy and strategic voting. He notes that parties have to pursue two different strategies: competition in the first round of voting and cooperation in the second round. He demonstrates empirically that a party is most likely to transfer its votes to the coalition partner in the second round of voting if the partner is likely to win. If the partner is likely to lose, then the number of transfers decreases, since voters would be wasting their vote. Thus, voters are more likely to vote strategically in the second round of the French system if they are sure that they can help the coalition partner win the constituency seat. Parties need to ensure that voters are confident that the coalition partner will win.

Schlesinger and Schlesinger (1998) argue that the French system has created four dominant parties that can form alliances of the left and right. The UDF and RPR on the right and PS and PC on the left generally agree to put forward one candidate in the second round of an election to ensure that one right or one left candidate can win a seat. Except in a few rare instances, the FN has been left out of these second-round alliances, making it difficult for the FN to win seats. Until the 1997 election, the UDF and RPR did not need the FN to win a plurality in the second round. In the case of the FN, Schlesinger and Schlesinger note that "[t]he striking discrepancy between the FN's ability to pile up protest votes and its ability to elect candidates or to hold onto elected officials reflects the FN's incapacity to execute any of the winning strategies implicit in dual-ballot elections" (Schlesinger and Schlesinger 1998, 75).

Cox's analysis of the SMDB electoral system (Cox 1997) indicates that it is difficult for voters to vote strategically in the first round, since it is more difficult to predict which candidate will make it into the second round. In this situation, left and right parties are more likely to act strategically by coordinating in the first round, by putting up only one candidate each. In this way, they can be assured that the left and right vote won't be split and their candidate will make it into the second round.

Based on the works cited earlier and Cox's predictions for the French system, it would be expected that the FN might be successful in winning votes in the first round of voting, but it would be strategically deserted in the second round if it is clear that the FN candidate cannot win the seat, and a vote for the FN would be wasted. The FN has had more success recently, getting over the 12.5% hurdle and being able to contest the second round. Since they tend to draw more votes away from the right than the left, the FN's increased success has made it difficult for right parties to follow their usual coalition strategies in both the first and second round. In the first round, the conservative right has had to agree on one candidate, so that they can be assured that a UDF or RPR candidate will make it into the second round.[3] This agreement occurred in 505 districts, as compared with only 11 districts where the left was able to agree on one candidate. In the second round, the right has refused to

---

[3] This does not keep other right or independent parties from fielding candidates.

cooperate with the FN, so they have risked losing to the left candidate if the FN is able to draw away enough votes from the right. In order for this strategy to work, the right must expect that the FN candidate will be strategically deserted by voters.

HYPOTHESIS 2: In an SMDB electoral system, a third party candidate will be strategically deserted in the second round if voters know that the candidate cannot win the seat or that the vote for the top two candidates will be close.

This hypothesis relies on the assumption that voter knowledge will influence strategic voting. Voters will have polling data available that will indicate if a third-party candidate can win a seat. This hypothesis will be tested in districts where three candidates contest the second round. I expect to find that the percentage of the vote received by the FN declines from the first round to the second round in those districts.

Germany – Electoral System

After World War II, Germany adopted a system of PR with half of the seats allotted by lists at the *Land* level and the other half determined by direct constituency votes. Each voter has two votes: the first for a candidate and the second for a party list. The distribution of seats is determined by the results of the second vote. Candidates who are elected through the first (constituency) vote are deducted from the party's overall list vote, so that the distribution of seats ends up being the same as a pure PR system. Germany has a 5% electoral threshold at the national level, or three constituency seats, to discourage the rise of extreme parties.

Despite the fact that Germany uses a PR system, it has a bipolar party system. Only three parties have been in government since World War II: the Christian Democrats (CDU/CSU), the Socialists (SPD), and the liberals or Free Democrats (FDP). In the past, the largest party has formed a coalition with the FDP to form a majority, with the exception of the grand coalition between the Christian Democrats and Socialists in 1966. In the 1998 election the Free Democrats maintained an electoral coalition with the CDU/CSU, and the SPD ended up forming a government with the Green Party. As noted earlier, Cox points out that the constituency vote in Germany makes it similar to the English system. A small party can't win a constituency seat because it will be strategically deserted. In recent elections, it has been difficult for parties like the radical right *Republikaner* to win second votes because of the need for the CDU/CSU and the FDP to form a coalition to ensure a majority, which I discuss in more detail next.

The 5% threshold increases the prospects for strategic voting, as voters may not be certain that their most-preferred party will qualify. This threshold is not sufficient, however, to prevent small parties from winning seats. The German Greens managed to enter the *Bundestag* in 1983, and the Party of Democratic Socialism (PDS) was able to win more than three constituency seats in 1994 to continue its presence in the *Bundestag*, despite falling below the 5% threshold at the national level.

Factionalism

The far right in Germany has been particularly prone to factionalism during its history. The National Democratic Party (NPD) has had consistent difficulties between different factions within the party, as described in detail in Chapter 2. For the *Republikaner*, factions formed around the more moderate Franz Schönhuber and the more fundamentalist activists in the party. As described in Chapter 2, both parties have had to deal with internecine splits between party leaders, which has led to a weaker and more radical leader being in control of the party. Unlike in the Austrian case, these leaders weren't able to consolidate power by getting rid of rivals. Clearly, this has had a negative impact on the ability to compete in the German party system.

Germany's radical right has not only dealt with factionalism within parties but also rivalry between parties. The *Republikaner* and NPD do not work together and tend to compete for the same voters, although the *Republikaner* has had more success than the NPD. A third party, the German People's Union (DVU), also has competed against the NPD and *Republikaner*. The DVU has been a personal vehicle for its founder, Gerhard Frey, and there has been little or no cooperation among these parties.

Coalition Structure/Strategy

Germany's two-vote system creates a particular incentive for small parties to campaign for second votes. Winning seats with the first vote is nearly impossible for small parties. For example, only one FDP member has won a constituency seat in the last 50 years. Several authors have written about the FDP's strategy of campaigning for the second vote in German elections. In his study of the 1965 and 1969 *Bundestag* elections, Stephen Fischer (1973) argues that voters tended to use their second vote to support small parties. Small parties such as the FDP and NPD or REP consistently get higher percentages of the second vote than the first vote. The larger parties tend to get a higher percentage of the first vote (constituency vote) than the second vote (party vote). Fischer argues that voters are not willing to "waste" their vote for a candidate of a small party in the first vote. Therefore, voters are more likely to vote sincerely for a party with their second vote.

Using material from FDP campaigns, Geoffrey Roberts shows that the FDP clearly campaigned for second votes using campaign slogans such as "rule of thumb '80 – second vote FDP" (quoted in Roberts 1988, 324). He points out that the FDP used this strategy when it was in coalition with the SPD and with the CDU/CSU. The difference between the percentage of the vote received by the FDP on the first and second votes is significant (more than 3.5 percentage points), particularly in three elections through 1987 in which the FDP was below 5% on the first vote. The FDP also was below 5% of the first votes in the 1994 election but received 6.9% of the second votes (see Table 6.1). Overall, the FDP gets a higher percentage of second votes than first votes, making its strategy of campaigning for second votes effective in maintaining its presence in the *Bundestag*.

In his article on vote-splitting in Germany, Eckhard Jesse concludes that "[t]he second vote is therefore quite consciously cast by 'splitters' for the second most desirable party, to make an appropriate coalition formation possible" (Jesse 1988, 121). Kathleen Bawn (1998) expands on this argument in her article on ticket-splitting in Germany. She argues

TABLE 6.1. *Percentage of the Vote Received in German Elections by Party*

Year	NPD/REP* 1st	NPD/REP* 2nd	CDU/CSU 1st	CDU/CSU 2nd	SPD 1st	SPD 2nd	FDP 1st	FDP 2nd	Green 1st	Green 2nd
1965	1.8	2.0	48.8	47.6	40.1	39.3	7.9	9.5	–	–
1969	3.6	4.3	46.6	46.1	44.0	42.7	4.8	5.8	–	–
1972	0.5	0.6	45.4	44.9	48.9	45.8	4.8	8.4	–	–
1976	0.4	0.3	48.9	48.6	43.7	42.6	6.4	7.9	–	–
1980	0.2	0.2	46.0	44.5	44.5	42.9	7.2	10.6	1.9	1.5
1983	0.2	0.2	52.1	48.8	40.4	38.2	2.8	7.0	4.1	5.6
1987	0.2	0.6	47.7	44.3	39.2	37.0	4.7	9.1	7.0	8.3
1990	1.7	2.1	45.7	43.8	35.2	33.5	7.8	11.0	4.4	3.8
1994	1.7	1.9	45.0	41.5	38.3	36.4	3.3	6.9	6.5	7.3

* NPD 1965–1987, REP 1990–1994.
Source: National election returns.

that voters in Germany respond rationally to incentives provided by the electoral system. The article focuses on voters' incentives to vote for different parties with their two votes. She notes that research has shown that "[s]econd-vote supporters of small parties do react to the incentive to not waste their vote in a district race" (Bawn 1998, 8). Bawn's analysis supports the argument that FDP voters do strategically choose the FDP with their second vote, and therefore the FDP's campaigning is effective. Jesse's and Bawn's analyses support the argument that German voters consciously choose a different party with their second vote to ensure the election of their preferred coalition.

Cox also notes that the electoral threshold in Germany has influenced the FDP's strategy (Cox 1997). The FDP has explicitly solicited second votes from voters to ensure that its alliance with the SPD or CDU/CSU can continue. Cox shows that this type of strategic calculation also affects Green voters, since the Green Party is seen as a possible coalition partner with the SPD. Cox's argument differs from those discussed earlier in that he argues that voters may be *locally strategic*, that is, they may take into consideration not only national-level coalition preferences, but also that the outcome in their local constituency may affect how they use their second vote. Using regression analysis, Cox shows that there is a significant negative relationship between the absolute difference in the constituency votes (first votes) for the top two candidates and the percentage of votes an FDP or Green candidate loses between the first and second votes. In other words, as the margin of victory of the constituency vote decreases, the FDP's and Green's loss of votes between the first and second vote increases. Voters are more likely to strategically desert their first choice and use their list vote for one of the top two parties (CDU/CSU or SPD) as the margin of victory decreases.

Each of these studies indicates that strategic voting plays a role in the coordination and strategies of at least the small German parties. Using the following hypothesis, I test to see if this type of coordination and strategic voting has an effect on the vote for the radical right; I look for evidence of strategic voting when a probable coalition partner is in danger of falling below the 5% hurdle.

HYPOTHESIS 3. A radical right party will be strategically deserted for a party that is part of a preferred coalition in districts where it is possible that the preferred coalition partner will fall below the threshold required to enter the legislature.

As shown by each of the authors discussed earlier, the FDP tends to get a higher percentage of second votes than first votes, particularly in elections where it is below the 5% hurdle in first votes. I test to see if there is a relationship in the percentage of second votes for the radical right and the FDP and how this relationship affects the vote for the radical right. I would expect to find a negative relationship between these variables if the radical right is being strategically deserted.

HYPOTHESIS 4: In districts where the difference in the vote between the top two parties is close, voters are more likely to vote strategically for a mainstream party and strategically desert the radical right.

This hypothesis refers to locally strategic voting as described in this section by Cox. Voters are more likely to use their second votes for their preferred party when the margin of victory between the top two parties is large. I test to see if the same type of strategic calculus is used by radical right voters.

6.3. EMPIRICAL EVIDENCE OF STRATEGIC VOTING AND STRATEGIC COORDINATION

In this section, I describe the results of recent elections in each country and test the hypotheses derived in the previous section. The hypotheses are based on the different electoral systems in each country; therefore the analysis is divided into sections by country. Using electoral data, I conduct simple tests to provide inferences as to the effects of strategic voting and strategic coordination on the success of radical right parties.

Austria

The vote for the two main parties in Austria has declined significantly since the 1986 election. Table 6.2 displays the share of the vote for each party from 1970 to 1999. The SPÖ's share of the vote has declined from a high of 51% in 1979 to a low of 34.9% in 1994. The ÖVP has shown a similar decline, dropping from 44.7% in 1970 to only 27.7% in 1994. Both parties have lost votes to the FPÖ and Green parties, but the ÖVP has had a much more severe decline than the SPÖ. The decline in the vote for the ÖVP and SPÖ has meant that neither party can govern alone, making a coalition necessary to form a majority.

The 1990 election in Austria highlights the difficulties the mainstream parties had in finding a strategy against the FPÖ. The ÖVP could have acted as the opposition party in the 1990 election to blunt the new message from the FPÖ and its charismatic new leader, Jörg Haider, but the SPÖ

TABLE 6.2. *Voting in Austria by Party (percentage)*

Year	SPÖ	ÖVP	FPÖ	Greens*	Liberals
1970	48.4	44.7	5.52	–	–
1971	50.0	43.1	5.45	–	–
1975	50.4	42.9	5.4	–	–
1979	51.0	41.9	6.06	–	–
1983	47.7	43.2	4.98	4.2	–
1986	43.1	41.3	9.7	5.9	–
1990	42.8	32.1	16.6	8.5	–
1994	34.9	27.7	22.5	7.31	5.97
1995	38.1	28.3	21.9	4.8	5.5
1999	33.2	26.9	26.9	7.4	n/a

* From 1983 to 1990 there were several Green parties.
Source: National election returns.

made motions early in the election process to hold out the prospect of a great coalition. The ÖVP did not turn down this option and ended up relinquishing the position of opposition party to the FPÖ. The FPÖ was able to take advantage of the situation and "[c]onsequently, the ÖVP not only lost arguing strength, but also forfeited its leadership role in terms of the opinion climate and declared electoral intentions" (Plasser and Ulram 1989, 72).

The SPÖ had the most popular chancellor candidate in 1990, Franz Vranitzky, and felt that a coalition with the ÖVP was the best option to take after the election, since it would control the governing coalition. The SPÖ tried to get as high a percentage of the vote as possible, to confirm its leadership of the coalition. The SPÖ had no reason to consider a coalition with the FPÖ, since that would only alienate party activists, and the ÖVP's decline ensured that the SPÖ would control the government.

In my 1997 interview with a strategist from the ÖVP, the strategist noted that one of the tactics of the SPÖ in the 1994 election was to tell voters that they shouldn't vote for the ÖVP because if it received a high enough percentage of the vote, it would form a coalition with Haider's FPÖ. Although this strategy wasn't particularly successful, the ÖVP's percentage of the vote has declined to the point where it had no chance of creating a government by itself.

The basic problem for the ÖVP is that it only has two choices for coalition partners, the SPÖ and the FPÖ. The ÖVP has difficulty attracting FPÖ voters because the FPÖ voters know that the ÖVP is unlikely to gain a majority, and so they may as well vote for their preferred party. As noted in Table 6.2, the vote for both main parties declined during the 1980s and 1990s, but the ÖVP has declined the most, receiving only 28.3% of the vote in the 1995 legislative election.

The mainstream parties' decline has meant a steady increase in the vote for the radical right. The FPÖ received 16% of the vote in the 1990 Austrian legislative election, nearly doubling its total from the previous election. The FPÖ has been able to take advantage of government scandals, and, despite a few scandals of its own, it has always managed to bounce back in the polls. The strategic actions of the mainstream parties have not kept the FPÖ from winning seats and votes.

The 1999 election brought the Freedom Party a new level of electoral success. Prior to the election, polls were showing the possibility that the Freedom Party might take over second place from the conservatives. A great deal of uncertainty surrounded the outcome, and the parties had little incentive to try to encourage strategic voting. Table 6.3 lists chronologically the coalition signals in the year prior to the 1999 election. None of the parties was giving any firm coalition signals prior to the election except for the SPÖ, which indicated that it would not go into a coalition with the Freedom Party. After the election, the ÖVP and the SPÖ had several months of coalition negotiations that eventually failed. The government that was formed by the ÖVP and the Freedom Party was highly controversial, but by avoiding signaling their coalition preferences the leaders of the ÖVP had the flexibility to go into discussions with both the SPÖ and the FPÖ to secure the best deal that they could.

TABLE 6.3. *Coalition Signals – Austria 1999*

Date	Signal (from : to)	Source	Article ID*
April 99	ÖVP: no signal but leaning toward SPÖ	Party Convention	042699NZZ
Sept. 99	SPÖ: minority govt. or ÖVP	Party Leadership	091499SZ
	ÖVP: opposition if third party	Party Leadership	091499SZ
	FPÖ: all combinations possible	Party Leadership	091499SZ
	GA: SPÖ	Party Leadership	092899TAGES
	SPÖ: not FPÖ, minority govt.	Party Leadership	100199SZ
	Election Oct. 3		

* LexisNexis® articles, ID = dates and newspaper; GA = Grüne Alternative (Green Alternative Party).
Source: LexisNexis®, 01/99 to 11/99.

In the end, the leader of the ÖVP became chancellor, despite the fact that the party came in third in the election. The fact that the Freedom Party didn't demand the chancellorship and didn't make Haider a part of the government shows how the Freedom Party was willing to compromise in the coalition negotiations in order to achieve its goal. Unlike some radical right parties, it was willing to work with the mainstream right in order to have an influence on government policy.

Austria – Data Analysis

To test hypothesis 1, I attempt to determine if the closeness of the vote at the district level between the two main parties has any effect on the vote for the FPÖ. If strategic voting were occurring, I would expect the vote for the FPÖ to be lower when the vote for the two main parties is close and the FPÖ vote to be higher when the two main parties are far apart. Since strategic voting is not likely to be occurring in Austria, I actually expect to find no relationship between the FPÖ vote and the difference in the vote for the SPÖ and ÖVP.

Table 6.4 lists the difference in the vote between the SPÖ and the ÖVP at the national level. There doesn't appear to be any relationship between the difference in the vote for the ÖVP and the SPÖ and the vote for the FPÖ. When the difference between the two mainstream parties was at its largest, 10.7% in 1990, the FPÖ received 16.6% of the vote. When the

TABLE 6.4. *Difference in the Vote for the Mainstream Parties in Austria vs. the FPÖ vote (percentage)*

Year	SPÖ Vote	ÖVP Vote	SPÖ–ÖVP Vote Difference	FPÖ Vote
1970	48.4	44.7	3.7	5.5
1971	50.0	43.1	6.9	5.5
1975	50.4	42.9	7.5	5.4
1979	51.0	41.9	9.1	6.1
1983	47.7	43.2	4.5	4.9
1986	43.1	41.3	1.8	9.7
1990	42.8	32.1	10.7	16.6
1994	34.9	27.7	7.2	22.5
1995	38.1	28.3	9.8	21.9
1999	33.2	26.9	6.3	26.9

Source: National election returns.

TABLE 6.5. *Relationship of FPÖ Vote
with Difference in Mainstream Party
Vote (absolute value)*

Pooled Data – *Länder* Level

	FPÖ Vote 1966–1999
Constant	0.111**
	(0.022)
[SPÖ–ÖVP]	0.067
	(0.052)
N	90

** Indicates significant at .05 level of confidence.

difference declined to 7.2% in 1994, the vote for the FPÖ increased to
22.5%. The vote for the FPÖ did not decrease, as would be expected with
strategic voting.

National-level data may be misleading, so I have also collected electoral
data from 1966 to 1999 at the *Land* level (10 elections). To test the
relationship between the vote for the FPÖ and the mainstream parties, I
have run a regression of the vote for the FPÖ on the absolute value of
the difference in the vote between the SPÖ and the ÖVP. Since there are
only 9 *Länder*, data from legislative elections from 1966 to 1999 have
been pooled into one regression. The results of the regression analysis
are displayed in Table 6.5 The results show that the coefficient for [SPÖ–
ÖVP] is not significantly different from zero, which indicates that there is
no relationship between the FPO vote and the difference in the SPÖ and
ÖVP vote at the district level.

This test indicates that the vote for the FPÖ is not affected by the
closeness of the vote between the two mainstream parties in Austria. This
result supports the hypothesis that the great coalition in Austria has kept
voters from strategically deserting the FPÖ. Aggregate analyses of this
nature are, however, problematic. Attempting to infer individual behavior
from aggregate data can lead to an ecological inference problem. In the
case of Austria, individual-level data are available from exit polls from
the 1999 legislative election.

Table 6.6 displays the number of voters who stated that they had voted
for a different party than the one that they had wanted to vote for originally. Of those surveyed, 724 of 3010 (24%) had considered voting for
another party. The first part of the table looks at the party voted for versus
the party the voter originally wanted. The second part looks at a series

TABLE 6.6. *Austrian 1999 Election Exit Poll – Strategic Voting? (raw numbers)*

Number of voters who stated they voted for a party other than their original choice: 724 of 3010 surveyed (24%)

Which party did you vote for?	Which party did you want originally?					
	SPÖ	ÖVP	FPÖ	LF	Greens	Total
SPÖ	13	24	50	21	56	164
ÖVP	26	3	53	28	47	157
FPÖ	53	49	5	7	13	127
LF	13	18	3	0	40	74
Greens	56	30	10	50	0	146
TOTAL	161	124	121	106	156	668

Why didn't you vote for the original party?	Which party did you want originally?					
	SPÖ	ÖVP	FPÖ	LF	Greens	Total
To weaken the FPÖ	4	2	15	3	19	43
against an ÖVP–FPÖ coalition	0	6	2	1	0	9
To strengthen another party	8	5	3	5	26	47
Wanted a change	17	10	1	2	2	32
Protest vote	16	8	3	0	3	30
Tactical vote	2	3	2	1	11	19
To strengthen the opposition	2	2	1	1	2	8
Foreigner policy	6	3	2	0	4	15
Too radical	0	0	18	2	3	23
Other party is better	6	7	10	13	12	48

Underlining designates larger numbers.
Source: FESSEL = Gfk. 1999.

of questions asked as to why the voter chose a different party. In each section, I have highlighted the numbers that stand out.

In the first part of the table it is interesting to note that every party had a significant number of supporters who ended up voting for a different party. Many voters who originally wanted to vote for the Freedom Party switched to the socialists and conservatives, but the Freedom Party also received votes from those who switched from the socialists and conservatives. The Greens and Liberal Forum (LF) also switched relatively equal numbers of voters. The Liberal Forum was the only party that had a much lower number of voters in this group (74) versus those who indicated an initial preference for the party (106).

When we look at the reasons why voters didn't vote for their original choice, the main reasons for not choosing the SPÖ were that they wanted a change or to be a protest voter. For the ÖVP, no reason stands out, but wanting a change got 10 responses. For those who had considered the Freedom Party, the reason was to weaken the FPÖ or because it was too radical. For the Greens it was to weaken the FPÖ or to strengthen another party. Only Green voters (11) said in any numbers that they were voting tactically. Considering the number of overall voters in the survey (3010) these numbers are very small. Unfortunately, I do not have comparable survey data for the other cases with which to compare these; but these numbers don't provide much evidence for strategic voting, consistent with my hypothesis. Voters do not appear to abandon the FPÖ because of the coalition strategies of the two mainstream parties. In the survey data described earlier, only 9 voters overall said that they were voting against an ÖVP–FPÖ coalition. Many voters did want to weaken the FPÖ (43), but this can be attributed to a simple dislike for the party or its leader. This confirms my hypothesis that strategic voting and strategic coordination have had little effect on the FPÖ vote, thus explaining its relatively high degree of success in tapping the potential radical right vote.

France

The French two-ballot electoral system and multi-party system make cooperation between parties necessary on the second ballot. Prior to the entry of the National Front, the left and right developed coordination strategies to ensure that voters would usually be faced with one candidate from the right and one candidate from the left in the second round of a legislative election. Since the National Front has had increased success, the right parties also have had to coordinate so that voters only have to choose one mainstream right candidate in the first round of the election.

Table 6.7 details election results in France from 1981 to 1997. The percentage of the vote that the mainstream parties have received in the first round of the double ballot has declined since 1981. The RPR and UDF have dropped from a combined 40.1% in 1981 to 23.4% in 1997. The PS has dropped from 36.3% in 1981 to 25.6% in 1997. However, the mainstream parties have not lost as much of the vote in the second round. Both the RPR/UDF and PS received between 30% and 55% of the vote, with the numbers fluctuating due to the alternation of the parties in government.

TABLE 6.7. *Percentage of the Vote Received in French Elections by Party*

| | First and Second Round | | | | | | | |
| | FN | | RPR/UDF | | PS | | PC | |
Year	1st	2nd	1st	2nd	1st	2nd	1st	2nd
1981	0.2	0	40.1	41.0	36.3	49.3	16.1	6.9
1986*		9.7		44.8		30.7		9.8
1988	9.7	1.1	37.7	46.8	36.4	49.1	11.3	3.1
1993	12.4	5.7	39.7	55.0	17.3	29.8	9.2	4.6
1997	14.9	5.6	23.4	46.0	25.6	38.9	9.9	3.8

* PR system used in this election, only one round contested.
Source: National election returns.

The FN's success in the mid-1980s came immediately after the right's loss to the socialists. The RPR began to focus on issues such as immigration, and this focus also helped to legitimize these themes for the FN. Marcus points out that in 1984, "[w]hile continuing to attack Le Pen himself, Chirac determined to bid for the Front's supporters by advocating a tougher line in immigration and crime" (Marcus 1995, 136).

The switch to proportional representation for the 1986 parliamentary elections forced all of the parties to differentiate themselves to gain the highest possible percentage of the vote. The mainstream right had to make a clear distinction between itself and the National Front. It avoided issues such as immigration and security that were the focus of the FN, and instead it focused on issues such as employment and its ability to handle cohabitation.[4] The mainstream right did not want to appear to be parroting the line of the FN. Although the right won the majority of votes in this election, the percentage of the vote received by the FN increased from 0.3% of the vote in 1981 to 9.6% in 1986.

The introduction of proportional representation helped the National Front by allowing it to win seats in the legislature. Voters knew that their votes would not be wasted, so they could vote for their preferred party. To avoid increased support for the FN in future elections, the new conservative government changed the electoral laws back to the two-ballot system.

---

[4] With Mitterrand of the Socialist Party as president, a conservative prime minister would create the first situation of cohabitation in France's Fifth Republic.

During the 1988 legislative election, the RPR and UDF joined in an electoral alliance called the *Union du Rassemblement et du Centre* (Union of the Rally and of the Center; URC) to avoid having to make electoral alliances with the FN. The URC stated that it would reject any deals with the FN. Le Pen threatened to run candidates in the second round in every district the FN could to dilute the right vote. After the first round, the conservatives were forced to ally with the FN or risk losing seats. The URC withdrew candidates in eight districts near Marseille so that the FN candidate would face the left candidate, instead of a three-way race. The FN reciprocated in eight other districts. However, the FN only won one seat, while the URC went into opposition with 40.5% of the vote. The FN deputy later resigned from the party, and the FN lost its only seat.

By the time of the 1993 legislative election, the Front had rebounded in local elections. The mainstream right refused to cooperate with the FN, forcing the FN to focus its campaign on the long-term prospects for the party. The FN's chances of gaining seats would continue to be slim as long as the RPR and UDF refused to ally with it at the district level. To keep FN voters from feeling that they were wasting their vote, the FN had to focus on a long-term strategy. Marcus notes that "Carl Lang compared the Front to the fabled tortoise, confident that it would ultimately catch the electoral hares – a strategy presumably for the long term" (Marcus 1995, 68).

Le Pen once again stated that as many FN candidates as possible would compete in the second round of voting. He campaigned against both the left and right, particularly since both sides had supported the Maastricht Treaty. Despite several "triangular" contests with FN candidates, the mainstream right ended up winning the election by a large margin (55% of the second-round vote), and the FN did not gain any seats in this election.

The 1997 legislative election gave the FN an opportunity to use its electoral strength against the mainstream right. I discuss the results of the election in more detail in the next section, but the 15% of the vote received by the FN was the party's best result in any election. The mainstream right lost control of the government despite using a strategy similar to one employed in the 1993 election.

The mainstream right took the FN's increased success into account in the 1997 election. To avoid falling below the required 12.5% level in the first round in a district, the UDF and RPR agreed to field one candidate in many districts. This strategy ensured the mainstream right party would be able to advance to the second round. In Table 6.8, I list the coalition signals in the year prior to the 1997 election. Unlike the Austrian case, the

TABLE 6.8. *Coalition Signals – France 1997*

Date	Signal (from : to)	Source	Article ID*
May 1996	RPR: UDF	Party Leadership	052096LesE
June 1996	PS: Republican Front against FN	Party Leadership	061896LM
	UDF: no alliance with FN		
December 1996	RPR: factions RPR, UDF	Party Leadership	120396LM
February 1997	Right: refuse Republican Front	Party Leadership	021597LM
	Left: single left candidate against FN. No Republican Front	Party Leadership	022797LM
March 1997	UDF/RPR: union	Party Leadership	031797LF; 031797LesE
	Right: refuse Republican Front	Party Leadership	031897LM; 032097LM; 032897LesE
	Right: refuse agreement with FN	Party Leadership	032197LM
	UDF: ban on FN	Party Member	032397AFP
	Right: refuse agreement with FN/refuse Republican Front	Party Leadership	032497LM

* LexisNexis® articles, ID = dates and newspaper.
Source: LexisNexis®, 03/1996 to 05/1997.

mainstream parties stated their preferences early and often. The UDF and RPR made it clear that they would go into coalition with each other and not work with the FN. They also made it clear that they would not join a "Republican Front" with the left in order to keep the FN from winning seats. These signals were clearly designed to suppress the vote for the FN, but the right also wanted to avoid the appearance of collusion with the left. Leaders feared that such a strategy may have pushed some of their more right-wing voters to the FN, as likely happened in Austria with its history of great coalitions.

Despite Le Pen's success in making it into the second round of the presidential election in 2002, the FN was only able to win 11% of the vote in the first round of the 2002 legislative election. The right's refusal to cooperate with the FN finally paid off, and the mainstream right won the majority of seats. An important strategy for the right in this election was to join together in a pre-electoral coalition called the Union for the Presidential Majority (UMP – *Union pour la Majorité Présidentiel*). By forming this coalition, the right could effectively avoid diluting its vote in the first round of the legislative election and tap into the voters' desire to avoid another period of cohabitation. As Colette Ysmal (2003) notes, 21% of those who had voted for Le Pen in the presidential election voted UMP in the legislative election.

With the exception of the 1988 election, leaders of the mainstream right parties have tried to isolate the FN by opposing any cooperation with the FN. However, the only hope the FN has of gaining seats in the national legislature is through alliances with the mainstream right. Strategists for the UDF and RPR emphasize that they are more willing to lose an election than ally with the FN. Although this may not appear to be a rational strategy, the mainstream right fears that an alliance with the FN would cost it a significant portion of center right voters who think that Le Pen is dangerous. In the face of the mainstream right's firm stance against alliances, it is difficult for the FN to translate votes into seats. In the French case, the actions of the mainstream parties have kept the FN from having success in terms of winning seats, despite the fact that it has been able to win up to 15% of the vote in the first round of legislative elections.

France – Data Analysis

The French case provides an opportunity to explore strategic coordination between parties in more detail. The increase in the FN's share of the vote has created a situation in which the mainstream right parties have had to pursue a new strategy. In past elections, the right and left parties made deals among themselves so that the candidate with the highest percentage in the first round would move on to the second round, and the other party would encourage its voters to transfer their votes. With the entry of the National Front, the mainstream right has had to put up only one candidate in the first round of the election to ensure that its candidate will get at least 12.5% of the vote in the first round and be able to contest the second round.

The hypothesis I test in this portion of the analysis depends on the FN getting a high enough percentage of the vote to make it into the second round of the election. The 1997 election is a good case to test strategic voting, due to the FN's success in making it into the second round in many districts. The electoral data from this election show that of 555 electoral districts in metropolitan France, the FN was above 12.5% of the vote in

TABLE 6.9. *France 1997 Election Results – FN vs. Left and Right*

	Averages					
	FN		Right		Left	
	1st	2nd	1st	2nd	1st	2nd
Overall N = 555	15.3	5.8	30.5	44.6	31.8	47.9
FN in N = 132	23.1	23.1	26.9	38.9	24.5	36.4
Right out N = 25	23.8	36.8	16.8	0	30.1	63.2
Left out N = 31	23.2	32.0	31.8	68.0	16.9	0
Three way N = 76	22.6	17.5	28.2	39.9	25.9	42.5

Source: National election returns.

133 districts after the first round and chose to contest 132.[5] The election campaign ended with the left winning 320 seats, the right 257, and the FN claiming only one seat.

To test hypothesis 2, I have divided the results for the FN, the right candidates, and the left candidates into five categories, as shown in Table 6.9. The percentages in the first row of the table (Overall) are the overall vote in the first and second round for each set of candidates. The second row (FN in) presents the percentage of the vote received in those districts where the National Front contested the second round. In the third (Right out) and fourth (Left out) rows, I have included the results for the districts where the right or left candidate dropped out in the second round. The final row (Three way) displays the results for the districts where all three candidates contested the second round.

It is interesting to note that the FN's share of the vote increased from the first round to the second round in those districts where it faced only one right or left candidate. The FN's vote increased the most when the right candidate dropped out of the second round (36.8% vs. 31.9% when the left candidate dropped out). This increase is due to the fact that more right voters chose the FN over a left candidate. However, the FN was able to win only one of these districts, since a large enough percentage

[5] The FN dropped out of one district to help a mainstream right candidate it favored.

of voters still chose the left candidate over the FN. In the districts where there was no right candidate in the second round, the left's vote increased to 63.2% in the second round, as compared to 47.9% overall. When there was no left candidate, the right's vote increased to 68.0% as compared with 44.6% overall.

In those districts where the race was between three candidates, the vote for the FN was less than in the first round. This would indicate that voters strategically deserted the FN in the second round, when there were two mainstream candidates in the race. There were 76 districts in which the FN faced candidates from both the left and right, and the FN did not win any of these contests. Forty-seven of these contests were won by the left, and 29 were won by the right. It would appear that the left benefited from the FN's determination to remain in the second round. The right in France paid a heavy price for its unwillingness to cooperate with the FN. However, this strategy was successful in preventing the FN from gaining seats, and in the long run it did not keep the right from winning overwhelmingly in the 2002 legislative election.

Despite calls to FN supporters to maintain support for the FN in the second round in the case of three-way contests, the percentage of the vote received by the FN in the second round dropped an average of 5% across all districts in three-way contests.[6] Without an alliance with one of the mainstream parties, voters know that an FN candidate cannot gain a high enough percentage of the vote to beat a mainstream candidate. Both the results from the first round of the election and survey evidence would be enough to convince FN voters to strategically desert their candidate. These results support the hypothesis that a third-party candidate will be deserted when voters know that the candidate cannot win the seat. Although they may have preferred the FN, the overall preference of more instrumental voters was for a right candidate to win.

The coordination on the part of the mainstream parties was critical in preventing the FN from winning legislative seats. Voters for the UDF or RPR did not have to worry about their candidate making it into the second round of the election, since they were only presented with one conservative candidate in most cases.

Although individual-level strategic voting plays a role in the French case, coordination between the parties played the most important role in preventing the FN from winning seats. The leadership of the mainstream

---

[6] There was little difference between districts where the right candidate won the seat or the left candidate won.

right parties in France has chosen a long-term strategy of keeping the FN out of the legislature. This strategy probably cost them several seats in the 1997 election.[7]

Germany

Prior to the *Republikaner*'s rise to prominence in the 1980s, the NPD was the main radical right party in Germany. Changes in the German economy and electoral alliances in the 1960s left an opening on the right for the NPD to exploit. The recession of 1966–1967 brought an end to the postwar *Wirtschaftswunder* (economic miracle). The CDU/CSU was in decline as the parties struggled to deal with the end of the Adenauer era. The FDP broke its coalition with the CDU in 1966, creating a crisis for the government. In December 1966, the CDU and SPD formed a "grand coalition" government. The grand coalition was part of the catalyst for a surge by the NPD in 1969. Since that time, the radical right has had little success in attracting voters away from the mainstream parties.

Table 6.1 displays electoral results in Germany from 1965 to 1994. The percentage of the vote received by the three mainstream parties has not declined to the same degree that it has in France, particularly on first votes. In terms of second votes, the CDU/CSU received around 46% of the vote in the late 1960s, and its share dropped to around 43% in the late 1980s and early 1990s. The SPD showed a decline of about 3 percentage points, from 39.3% in 1965 to 36.4% in 1994, and its percentage of the vote increased to 40.93% in the 1998 election. The FDP vote has ranged from a low of 5.8% in 1969 to a high of 11% in 1990. The radical right has only been close to the 5% electoral threshold in 1969, when it received 4.3% of the vote. Since that election, the highest percentage the *Republikaner* has received is 2.1% in 1990.

When the NPD first began to gain representation in the state-level elections, the mainstream parties' main concern was how these electoral gains looked to the foreign press. The CDU's response to the NPD was to formulate a new action program in 1968, which came to be known as the Berlin Program, to differentiate itself from its coalition partner. As Pridham notes, "In the new programme much more space was devoted to economic and social policy at the expense of foreign policy, so demonstrating the party's awareness of social change" (Pridham 1977, 180).

---

[7] This point is difficult to prove, since we cannot know what the election results would have been if they had cooperated with the FN.

Despite this new program, the CDU would lose the election, with the SPD gaining a solid majority in the legislature and the NPD receiving only 4.3% of the vote. The grand coalition government probably helped the NPD increase its vote share, but the 5% threshold kept the NPD from gaining seats in the legislature. After the disappointment of the 1969 election, party factionalism led to a breakdown in support for the NPD.

With the decline of the NPD, the radical right did not become a factor again until the 1980s and the rise of the *Republikaner*. In 1987, the CDU/CSU and FDP coalition had been in government since 1983. As Karl Cerny notes, "[T]he CDU/CSU was now the established government and showed the wear and tear of having responsibility for public policy; the SPD, as the opposition, could criticize without having to demonstrate the efficacy of its alternative policies" (Cerny 1990, 239). Factions within the CDU argued that the party needed to move to the right to cover its flank in case the *Republikaner* was able to gain a following. Others argued that the party should worry about its left flank and try to gain votes from the SPD.

The CDU/CSU was in a strong position to prevent the *Republikaner* from increasing its vote share in 1987. The *Republikaner*'s main stronghold was in Bavaria, where the CSU could move to the right of its coalition partner without fear of the coalition losing its share of the vote at the national level. The CSU's strength in Bavaria left it fairly immune to attacks from the left. Also, the 5% threshold made it difficult for the *Republikaner* to be a real threat to the CDU/CSU. The party could ignore the issues raised by the *Republikaner* and focus on the recent improvements in the economy. The SPD, in the meantime, had more to worry about from its left flank. The Greens were becoming a much stronger party, making it costly for the SPD to move to the right to appeal to voters from the CDU/CSU and FDP coalition while retaining its traditional left base. Although the CDU share of the vote decreased in this election, most of that loss appears to have been to the FDP. Table 6.1 indicates that the FDP received 9.1% of the second votes, an increase of 2% from the previous election, while both the CDU/CSU and SPD declined.

The fall of the Berlin Wall in 1989 and unification overshadowed the local-level successes of the *Republikaner* from 1987 to 1990. The *Republikaner* had tried to be the party of unification. After unification occurred, the party had to scramble to find new themes and attract voters in the East. Despite high levels of xenophobia in the East, the *Republikaner* was not able to organize well, and it fared poorly in the East during the 1990 legislative elections. The *Republikaner* had a difficult time planning its campaign in the East and was not allowed to campaign at all in Saxony, due to restrictions placed on extreme parties during that post-unification election. The *Republikaner* only received 2% of the vote. However, this was a higher percentage of the vote than it would receive in the 1994 election.

The inability of the *Republikaner* to gain votes in the face of a strong coalition between the Christian Democrats and the FDP had a strong impact on the party's internal cohesion. The *Republikaner* had some success in local elections prior to the 1994 legislative election. However the *Republikaner* was unable to continue that success, receiving only 1.9% of the vote in the 1994 legislative election, compared with the 10% of the vote it had received in the Baden-Württemberg state election in 1992. The party ran into major factional difficulties immediately prior to the election and the party's leader, Franz Schönhuber, resigned. Since that time, the *Republikaner* has had difficulty mounting a campaign at the national level.

The 1998 election was another disaster for the radical right, but it also indicates some of the intricacies of coalition signaling in the German case. The signals made during the year prior to the election are displayed in Table 6.10. From early on, polls were showing a close election between the SPD and CDU/CSU, with neither being able to win a majority of the seats in the *Bundestag*. Analysts predicted that the parties would have to go into a grand coalition. Only the FDP was willing to make a clear coalition signal, indicating that it would be willing to go into a coalition only with the CDU/CSU. The SPD wanted to avoid signaling a coalition with the Greens because it might have alienated more-moderate voters.

The *Republikaner* had no credible claim for a role in government, or even to break the 5% threshold in this environment. However, the FDP had to ensure that it received enough votes to get above the threshold; that provided an incentive for it to declare its coalition preferences. Strategic voting was much more of a factor for the FDP than for the radical right in Germany. As I show in the next section, the FDP's need to win votes to stay in a coalition with the CDU caused it to pursue a strategy that indirectly led to the radical right winning a lower percentage of the vote in more-contested districts.

Germany – Data Analysis

As discussed in the previous section, studies have made it clear that voters in Germany do vote strategically for the FDP on the second ballot.

TABLE 6.10. *Coalition Signals – Germany 1998*

Date	Signal (from : to)	Source	Article ID*
Early 1998	Grand coalition (continues until election day)	News media, election surveys	041898SZ; 051698SZ; 062098SZ; 071898SZ
April 1998	SPD: debate	Party leadership	040498SZ; 041698FAZ
	CDU: danger SPD/GB90, no grand coalition	Party leadership	042198FAZ
June 1998	FDP: CDU	Party convention	062798SZ
	CSU: no grand coalition	Party leadership	062898SZ; 063098SZ
July 1998	GB90: SPD	Party leadership	072998AP
August 1998	FDP: not SPD	Party leadership	081698AP
	SPD: no signal	News media	081798Focus
	CDU: not SPD and spreading fear of SPD/GB90	Party leadership (but internal disagreement)	081798Focus
September (before election)	SPD: no signal FDP: CDU GB90: SPD CDU: not SPD (with Kohl)	News media	090298Woche; 091498FAZ; 092598FAZ
September (after election)	SPD: GB90	Party leadership	092898SZ; 092998SZ

* LexisNexis® articles, ID = dates and newspaper; GB 90 = Greens and Bundnis '90.
Source: LexisNexis®, 04/98 to 10/98.

If they are voting for the FDP, then another party is losing votes. To a certain extent, these votes are coming from CDU/CSU voters who might otherwise choose the *Republikaner* with their second vote, but they also may be coming from *Republikaner* voters who prefer a CDU/CSU–FDP coalition. Based upon hypothesis 3, I expect that the vote for the *Republikaner* will be negatively related to the vote for the FDP in the 1990 and 1994 elections.

Hypothesis 4 indicates that the *Republikaner* will get a higher percentage of the vote when the right or left is certain to win a seat. Voters should be more likely to vote for a small party when the vote for the mainstream parties is not close. Since their vote is not likely to be decisive, they do not need to vote strategically. If this is happening in the German case, there

TABLE 6.11. *Relationship of the Vote for the Radical Right with the FDP in West Germany*

	REP 1990	REP 1990 (FDP <5%)	REP 1994
Constant	0.037**	0.059**	0.019**
	(0.004)	(0.013)	(0.002)
FDP 2nd Vote	−0.128**	−0.446**	0.016
	(0.038)	(0.179)	(0.029)
R^2	4.5%	11.7%	0.1%
N	248	49	248

** Indicates significant at .05 level of confidence.

should be a positive relationship with the difference in the CDU/CSU and SPD vote and the vote for the *Republikaner*.

To test the hypotheses, I have run a series of regressions of the vote for the radical right (the dependent variable) on the vote for the FDP and the absolute difference in the vote between the CDU/CSU and the SPD. I have chosen the 1990 and 1994 elections because these are the first two national elections the *Republikaner* contested. The data used for the analysis are the electoral results at the district level. Since the *Republikaner* was not allowed to campaign in portions of East Germany, I have only included results from the West, leaving a total of 248 electoral districts. Also, I am only using the second vote, since this vote determines the number of seats to be divided between the parties, and the majority of first votes go to the SPD and CDU/CSU.

In the case of the FDP vote, I have run three different regressions (Table 6.11). The first two are from the 1990 election. The first tests the overall relationship between the *Republikaner* vote and the FPD vote. Hypothesis 3 specifies that the radical right will be strategically deserted in districts where the FDP might fall below the 5% threshold, so I also have tested the relationship in districts where the FDP was below 5% of first votes.[8] There is a significant negative relationship between the second vote for the *Republikaner* and the second vote for the FDP. This relationship indicates that the *Republikaner* tends to get a lower percentage of the vote as the FDP vote increases. The second column in Table 6.11 indicates that this relationship is stronger in districts where the FDP is below 5% of the first vote. This stronger relationship supports the hypothesis that

[8] This is similar to the analysis used by Cox 1997, 82–83.

TABLE 6.12. *Relationship of the Vote for the Radical Right with the Difference in the Vote for the CDU and SPD in West Germany*

	NPD 1969	REP 1990	REP 1994
Constant	0.047[**]	0.014[**]	0.016[**]
	(0.002)	(0.001)	(0.001)
[CDU-SPD] 2nd	−0.022[**]	0.068[**]	0.031[**]
Vote	(0.008)	(0.008)	(0.006)
R^2	2.5%	21.5%	9.4%
N	248	248	248

[**] Indicates significant at .05 level of confidence.

the *Republikaner* is strategically deserted in districts where the FDP is in danger of falling below the 5% threshold.

The relationship with the vote for the FDP disappears in the 1994 election. I was not able to do the second part of the regression for the FDP with the 1994 data because the FDP was below 5% of the first vote in almost every district, so the results of the regression would be the same. Hypothesis 3 is not supported in the 1994 election. The closeness of the vote between the CDU/CSU and SPD in the 1994 election affected voters' strategies in this election.

I also test Hypothesis 1 with data from the 1969 German election. As in the Austrian case, I expect to find no relationship between the vote for the NPD and the absolute difference between the CDU/CSU and SPD vote, since the two parties were in a grand coalition prior to this election. The results of the bivariate regression analyses are displayed in Table 6.12.

The relationship of the radical right vote and the difference in the mainstream party vote is displayed in Table 6.12. The results for the NPD in 1969 are displayed in the first column. The regression analysis indicates a significant *negative* relationship between the vote for the NPD and the difference in the vote for the CDU/CSU and SPD. Although the result is significant, this is the opposite of what we would expect if strategic voting were occurring. The impact also is rather small, indicating a 0.2% decrease in the vote for the NPD as the difference in the vote for the two main parties' increases.

The results are quite different for the 1990 and 1994 elections that are displayed in the second and third columns of Table 6.12. There is a significant positive relationship with the REP vote and the difference between the CDU/CSU and SPD vote. The relationship is weaker in the

1994 election but is still significant. These results indicate that the *Republikaner* vote is lower in districts where the vote for the top two parties is close. Voters in these districts strategically desert the *Republikaner* for a mainstream party when their votes are more likely to have an impact on the end result.

The weaker result in Table 6.12 for the 1994 election may help explain the lack of a relationship between the *Republikaner* vote and the FDP vote in the 1994 election. The vote for the *Republikaner* was weaker overall in 1994, and it may simply be more difficult to find evidence of strategic behavior at the district level.

At least in the 1990 election, the results for the German case provide support for my hypotheses. However, they do not provide firm evidence of strategic voting. Without more-specific data, it is hard to prove that voters who preferred the *Republikaner* chose to vote for other parties. It is clear, however, that the FDP generally benefited from strategic voting on the second ballot.

Strategic voting in Germany appears to be driven by the coalition structure that has dominated German politics since World War II. The CDU/CSU and SPD coalitions with the FDP have been the main governing coalitions. The Green Party has managed to make itself a viable coalition partner on the left and has been rewarded with seats in the *Bundestag* and a place in the coalition government with the SPD in 1998. The FDP has consolidated its position on the right, leaving little room for another small party to be considered as a coalition partner for the CDU/CSU. The *Republikaner* has not been able to build itself into a viable coalition partner, and in 1990 this inability was translated into a lower percentage of the vote in districts where coalition strategy induced instrumental voters to vote strategically.

6.4. CONCLUSION

Strategic voting and strategic coordination have had an important effect on the ability of radical right parties to win votes and seats in France and Germany. The mainstream right parties have had to follow strategies that would ensure strategic behavior on the part of voters. The data analyses presented support the hypotheses developed in section III. In the Austrian case, and Germany in 1969, there is little evidence that strategic voting had as much of a negative impact on the ability of radical right parties to win votes and seats as in Germany in other election years.

I have provided evidence that coordination by the mainstream parties in France and coalition strategy in Germany can induce strategic voting, and that this does have an effect on the vote for the radical right. The electoral systems in France and Germany have made it easier for the mainstream parties in those countries to keep the radical right from winning legislative seats. The parties' strategies induce voters to make strategic choices in the voting booth, rather than simply choosing their preferred party.

Differences in electoral systems can help to provide an explanation for the difference in the level of success of radical right parties. Although it plays an important role, it is not just the electoral threshold in Germany that suppresses the vote for the *Republikaner*. The coalition between the FDP and the Christian Democrats discouraged voters from casting their second vote for the *Republikaner*. It has been difficult for the party to find a strategy to overcome this disadvantage. The *Republikaner* has not been much of a threat since the party's success in the European Parliament election of 1989. The *Republikaner*'s difficulties in gaining vote share have probably helped to keep the party factionalized. The departure of the party's leader, Franz Schönhuber, left the party with a new leader, Rolf Schlierer, who has been unable to work with other radical right parties and improve the party's electoral position.

In France, the FN continued to make gains at the local level until the split between the followers of Le Pen and of Bruno Mégret. The mainstream parties' coalition strategies do not work as well at the regional level (arguably, due to the proportional nature of regional elections). The French right faced a major crisis during the regional elections in 1998,[9] and Le Pen's showing in the 2002 presidential election caused concern for strategists on the right. Despite this, the mainstream right parties have maintained a cohesive strategy to keep the FN out of the national legislature in the long term, and this strategy paid off in the 2002 legislative elections in which they won a majority in the French Assembly.

---

[9] Several regional mainstream right candidates allied with the National Front and were forced to resign from their parties.

7

Extending the Model

Denmark

The profile of the radical right (RR) in Europe was heightened by the election of November 20, 2001, in Denmark. The Social Democrats (SD) were voted out, and a coalition led by the Liberal Party of Denmark (LP) was voted in. As with most recent Danish governments, this was a minority government, and as the LP had declared prior to the election, it was supported by the far-right Danish People's Party (DPP). Although it was not an official part of the government, it was clear that the DPP's positions on issues such as immigration were going to have a major impact on this government's policies.

It can be argued that the cases of France, Germany, and Austria present unique types of electoral systems that have led to the specific outcomes described herein. It is not clear, then, whether the same results would hold for another case that did not have these institutional idiosyncrasies (i.e., a two-vote system in France, a 5% threshold in Germany, and the great coalition tradition in Austria). In order to determine if the model I have developed makes sense in a broader context, I have chosen Denmark as a test case. The institutional differences in Denmark are that there is a pure proportional representation (PR) system (unlike France and Germany), and the mainstream parties have alternated in power (unlike Austria); thus this case provides additional variation on both the dependent and independent variables.

The Danish party system, however, does have its own unique characteristics. The main difference between Denmark and the other cases in this book is the predominance of minority governments. Kaare Strom's (1990) book on minority governments gives a thorough account of the rationality of minority governments; therefore I will not go into a full explanation of minority governments here. What is important in this case is the impact of minority government coalition formation on voter expectations. As in the Austrian case, coalition formation has not had a negative impact on the vote for the radical right in Denmark.

The rise of the Danish People's Party and the party it was originally a part of, the Progress Party, began during the mid-1970s. The Progress Party started out as an anti-tax party but, like the Austrian Freedom Party, it took on an anti-immigrant tone during the 1980s. The People's Party is also opposed to Denmark being part of the European Union. This Euroskepticism, nationalism, and anti-immigrant rhetoric of the Danish People's Party clearly puts it in the same category as the other radical right parties examined in this study.

The radical right in Denmark has been a force in Danish politics since Mogens Glistrup's Progress Party won 15% of the vote in the 1973 election, which saw the Danish party system go from four to seven competitive parties. In the 1998 election, despite being split into two parties, the Danish People's Party and the Progress Party managed to get a combined total of 9.8% of the vote. Although support for the Progress Party has declined, the Danish People's Party has managed to maintain levels of support of up to 15% in opinion polls since the 1998 election (Widfeldt 2000), and it received 12% of the vote in the 2001 legislative election. Danish election results are displayed in Table 7.1.

Denmark is a case where the actual number of immigrants should have had little effect on the vote for the radical right in the 1970s, since immigrants made up only 2% of the population and most were from other Scandinavian countries. Again, the Progress Party began as an anti-tax party and was successful prior to any significant immigration from Eastern Europe, Asia, and Africa. However, the number of foreigners in the country increased from less than 2% in the early 1970s to approximately 5% of the population in 2001. Immigration has now become a major issue in Denmark, with many mainstream party leaders taking a hard line on issues such as asylum seekers and family reunification.

Table 1.2 laid out the different variables used to explain the success of the radical right. In the case of Denmark, every variable was considered to be positive. That is, the radical right in Denmark has a strong, charismatic leader; has been able to attract the right kind of voters; and has not been hurt by strategic voting. The Danish case is very similar to the Austrian case. Like the Freedom Party in Austria, the split between

TABLE 7.1. *Party Support in General Elections, 1971–2001 (percentage)*

Year	LP	CPP	CrP	RV	SD	SPP	PP/DPP*	VS/UL**
1971	15.6	16.7	2.0	14.4	37.3	9.1		1.6
1973	12.3	9.2	4.0	11.2	25.6	6.0	15.3	1.5
1975	23.3	5.5	5.3	7.1	29.9	6.0	13.6	2.1
1977	12.0	8.5	3.4	3.6	37.0	3.9	14.6	2.7
1979	12.5	12.5	2.6	5.4	38.3	5.9	11.0	3.7
1981	11.3	14.5	2.3	5.1	32.9	11.3	8.9	2.7
1984	12.1	23.4	2.7	5.5	31.6	11.5	3.6	2.7
1987	10.5	20.8	2.4	6.2	29.3	14.6	4.8	1.4
1988	11.8	19.3	2.0	5.6	29.8	13.0	9.0	0.6
1990	15.8	16.0	2.3	3.5	37.4	8.3	6.4	1.7
1994	23.3	15.0	1.8	4.6	34.6	7.3	6.4	3.1
1998	24.0	8.9	2.5	3.9	36.0	7.5	7.4	2.7
2001	31.3	9.1	2.3	5.2	29.1	6.4	12.0	2.4

* 1971–1994 Progress Party, 1998–2001 Danish People's Party.
** 1971–1988 VS (Left Socialists), 1990–2001 Unity List (Left Socialists, Greens, and Communists).
Source: national election returns.

the more pragmatic Danish People's Party and the more liberal Progress Party actually allowed the leader of the DPP to consolidate control and get rid of more liberal and/or extreme elements of the party. Also, the DPP has benefited from the combination of a PR system and the lack of a mainstream party coalition strategy that was able to suppress the vote for the radical right.

In this chapter, I explore the Danish party and electoral systems in order to determine if the theories I have developed in regard to strategic voting help to explain the success of the radical right in Denmark. I begin by describing the development of Danish Radical Right parties and the types of voters they have attracted. I then explain the electoral system in Denmark and empirically test for the impact (or lack thereof) of strategic voting. I conclude with a discussion of the country-specific factors that have influenced the success of the radical right in Denmark.

7.2. BACKGROUND

In this section, I describe the contours of the Danish party system. I then describe the development of the radical right in Denmark, its policy positions, and the types of voters who are attracted to these parties. As with the previous cases, I conducted interviews with the radical right and main-stream parties in Denmark, and I summarize those interviews. This section concludes with a summary of the impact of foreigners and unemployment on the vote for the radical right in Denmark.

The Danish Party System

Like most countries with proportional representation, Denmark has a multi-party system. The main parties on the left are the Social Democrats (SD) and the Socialist People's Party (SPP). On the right the main parties are the Liberal Party of Denmark (LP) and the Conservative People's Party (CPP). Other smaller, center parties that have had varying influence on the party system over time include the Christian People's Party (CrP), the Center Democrats (CD), and the Radical Liberals (RL). On the extremes of the party system are the radical right Progress Party (FP) and the Danish People's Party (DPP) and, on the left, the Red-Green Unity List (UL).

As Ole Borre and Jørgen Andersen (1997) note, the Danish party system is a good example of Lipset and Rokkan's "freezing" hypothesis (Lipset and Rokkan 1967). The three main parties in the Danish system, the Social Democrats, the Liberal Party of Denmark, and the Conservative People's Party, have not changed since the 1920s. These parties have maintained a monopoly on the position of prime minister through the election of 2001. The electoral "earthquake" of 1973 caused a steep decline in the combined support of the three parties (see Figure 7.1), but that support rebounded quickly, and they have remained at close to 70% of the vote in the last four elections.

The Radical Right in Denmark

The history of the current radical right in Denmark begins with the electoral "earthquake" of 1973. In this election, there was a temporary shift away from the mainstream parties on the left to parties on the right, including the more extreme Progress Party. Tax lawyer Mogens Glistrup formed his party in 1972 as a form of tax protest. He claimed he had paid no taxes and that tax evaders were heroes (Widfeldt 2000). In recent party literature, the FP states that "the party has to this day continued the battle against the income tax, public bureaucracy, and other threats to individual liberty" (Progress Party 2001, 1).

According to Lars Bille (2001), by 1973 the Danish political parties had all moved to the center left, and there was an opportunity for parties to

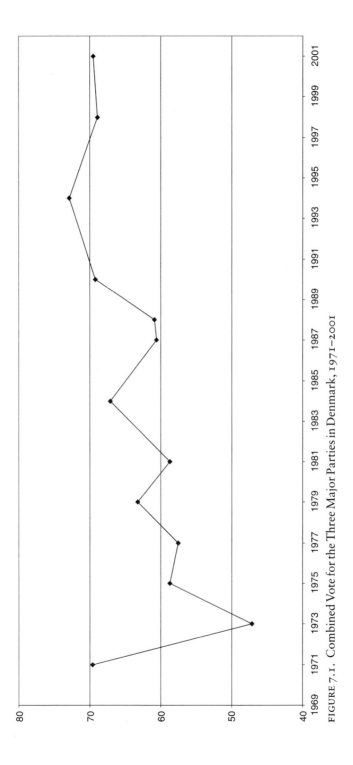

FIGURE 7.1. Combined Vote for the Three Major Parties in Denmark, 1971–2001

enter the system on the right. Several new parties gained representation in the Danish parliament in this election, including the Progress Party, which gained 15.9% of the vote. As Moshe Maor describes, "The Progress Party positioned itself as a popular movement operating against the 'old' parties" (Maor 1998, 28).

After this election, the Progress Party was unable to achieve the same result. Glistrup wasn't particularly interested in building a traditional party organization. The party was predictably hit by many internal splits between those who wanted to pursue cooperation with the mainstream parties (the pragmatists) and those who wanted the party to stand on its own (the fundamentalists). Glistrup was sentenced to three years in prison for tax fraud in 1983, which left the party in the hands of the pragmatists led by Pia Kjærsgaard (Widfeldt 2000).

Glistrup returned to a party that he no longer controlled in 1987 and was eventually expelled from the national executive of the party in 1991. Despite the marginalization of Glistrup, the pragmatists still struggled for control of the party. The differences between the two groups ultimately led to the party splitting into two parties: the Progress Party, which elected Kirsten Jacobsen as the party leader, and the Danish People's Party, led by Pia Kjærsgaard (Andersen and Bjørklund 2000). Unlike the split in Austria, the liberals remained in the tax-focused Progress Party, and the new DPP included the party members who were oriented toward immigration politics as their main issue. The Progress Party fared relatively poorly in the 1998 election, earning only 2.4% of the vote and four seats in parliament. Mogens Glistrup took over party leadership again for the 2001 election, but the FP was only able to get 0.6% of the vote, far below the 2% threshold for seats.

The DPP has had the upper hand since the 1998 election, and, despite the split, the party has done well in opinion polls. The DPP has maintained a rather strident anti-immigrant stance, but it also has been considered as a possible coalition partner by the conservative parties, and in 2001 the DPP agreed to support the minority government led by Prime Minister Anders Fogh Rasmussen of the Liberal Party of Denmark.

Policy Positions

As noted in the previous section, the Progress Party started out as an anti-tax crusade by Mogens Glistrup. The party didn't turn its attention to the immigration issue until 1979. However, the issue did not become an important one until the late 1980s, as the number of asylum seekers in Denmark increased dramatically from 800 in 1983 to 4700 in 1988. Glistrup began making comments about Muslims in Denmark and used the slogan, "Make Denmark a Muslim Free Zone" (quoted in Andersen and Bjørklund 2000, 205). At the time Pia Kjærsgaard was critical of such statements and wanted to keep criticism of immigrants "within socially acceptable limits" (Andersen and Bjørklund 2000, 205).

Kjærsgaard's split from the Progress Party gave her the ability to pursue the immigration issue in the way that she felt would attract voters, as well as to set up a hierarchical party structure that could be more "professional" than the Progress Party (Hermansson 2001). The Danish People's Party fits well into the criteria described in Chapter 2 that I use to define the radical right. The party clearly takes positions that are similar to those taken by the radical right in Austria, France, and Germany. The DPP is nationalistic, as shown in the party program: "The Danish People's Party's primary goal is to re-establish Denmark's independence and freedom and to protect the existence of the Danish nation and the Danish monarchy" (People's Party 2001, 1).

The DPP is clearly an anti-immigrant party. In its party program, it states that "Denmark is not, and has never been a country intended for immigration and the Danish People's Party disagrees with the statement that Denmark will develop into a multiethnic society" (People's Party 2001, 2). The DPP also has come out against the European Union and the Monetary Union. In fact, it states that the party is "deeply opposed to the European Union" (People's Party 2001, 3).

One difference with the Danish People's Party is that it has not tried to distance itself from the party system as much as have the RR parties in France, Germany, and Austria. The DPP sees cooperation with other parties in parliament as an important way of pursuing its agenda. Although it is not an official part of the government, the liberal/conservative minority government that formed after the 2001 election accepted the support of the DPP to form voting majorities in parliament.

Who Votes for the Radical Right in Denmark?

When the Progress Party first crashed onto the scene in 1973, its main appeal was as an anti-tax party. The party was attractive to older, self-employed males. Over time, the Progress Party attracted more workers and younger voters to its ranks. The Danish People's Party has continued the evolution to a working-class party.

TABLE 7.2. *Denmark 1998 Legislative Election Percentage of Social Group by Party (parties that won seats)*

	Unity List	RL	SPP	SD	LP	CPP	DPP
Gender							
Male	2.5	4.5	7.1	28.2	26.2	10.0	7.4
Female	3.6	3.8	9.3	29.0	20.2	9.5	4.9
Education							
School/Basic	3.0	3.7	7.9	30.3	21.9	5.9	7.1
Completed	0.9	1.5	4.6	32.8	25.9	9.4	8.8
University or Higher	5.4	7.7	12.6	22.1	21.8	14.6	1.9
Profession							
Farmers	0.0	0.0	0.0	0.0	65.7	2.9	8.6
Self-Employed	0.0	1.3	5.1	7.7	24.4	24.4	12.8
White-Collar	3.3	5.7	11.5	27.6	22.2	11.0	4.2
Blue-Collar	3.4	2.1	7.9	36.2	19.7	3.6	8.1
Student, Apprentice	7.9	9.7	14.1	20.3	17.2	7.5	4.0
Not Working	0.8	2.3	3.3	32.0	26.6	12.9	6.6
Age							
18–24	6.5	9.6	10.0	17.8	23.5	7.8	3.5
25–34	4.1	4.6	8.4	23.2	24.6	11.4	7.0
35–44	2.5	3.0	11.7	32.2	19.5	5.1	6.3
45–59	3.5	4.6	11.2	31.9	20.7	8.4	5.4
60–69	1.5	3.3	5.5	34.2	18.9	11.6	8.7
≥70	1.4	1.9	2.2	29.3	31.0	13.9	5.4
TOTAL	3.1	4.2	8.2	28.7	23.2	9.8	6.1
N	61	83	164	573	463	195	122

Source: Danish Election Survey 1998; results are weighted to adjust for demographic variance between survey and population.

The types of voters attracted to the Danish People's Party tend to be men without higher education. Data from the *Danish Election Survey 1998* (Table 7.2) indicate that the DPP gets 7.4% of all male voters (higher than the 6.1% of DPP voters in the poll) and only 4.9% of women voters. The DPP has not replaced the Social Democrats or the Socialist People's Party as the party of the workers. However, its electorate is disproportionately from the blue-collar sector (8.1% blue-collar workers vs. 6.1% of the electorate). The party also attracts a relatively high percentage of the self-employed (12.8%). This distribution is very similar to the proportions received by other radical right parties, particularly that of the French FN in 1997 (see Table 3.11).

In comparison with other radical right parties, what stands out in the case of the DPP electorate is the level of education. Its voters are much less likely to have a university education than any of the other radical right parties in this study, with the exception of the German parties, which get a much lower percentage of the vote overall. Despite this difference, the similarities between the electorate of the Danish People's Party and those of the radical right in Austria, France, and Germany are clearly greater than the differences.

Denmark Interviews

I conducted interviews with the Danish People's Party and the mainstream parties in Denmark in August 2001.

The DPP responded to my questions via email rather than granting an in-person interview, so I have the actual text of its response, which was in English. As with other radical right parties, it sees immigration as the most important problem facing Denmark,

> Denmark is currently being swamped by so-called refugees who claim their right to occupy Danish territory. We do not accept that right. The Danish People's Party is against immigration. We want to put a stop to permanent residence permits for foreigners. We want to put a stop to the granting of Danish citizenships. . . . All in all we want to preserve Denmark as the home of the Danish people.
> (Danish People's Party, July 2001)

The party also was very clear on its position on Europe: "The Danish People's Party is against the European Union and tries to prevent any form of constitution or initiatives which leads to a more tight union."

The DPP also has been very clear about its willingness to support a government coalition. Although it has "sometimes sided with the Social Democrats and Socialist Peoples Party" at the local level, it has a strong preference for a government consisting of the Danish Liberal Party and the Conservative People's Party. This willingness to consider working with the mainstream right is similar to the positions taken by the Freedom Party in Austria.

The mainstream parties did not seem to have a consistent strategy for dealing with the DPP. On the left, they wanted to deal with issues of integrating already-resident immigrants and to ignore the DPP. On the right, they tended to speak against the radical right and its alarmist use of immigration statistics. There was some concern that the DPP might be in a position to support the next government and use its influence to impact immigration policy, which did indeed happen after the election in November 2001.

Unemployment, Foreigners, and the Radical Right Vote

In a study of monthly opinion data from 1980 to 1990, Christopher J. Anderson (1996) examined the impact of economics, politics, and foreigners on the support for the Progress parties in Denmark and Norway. Anderson found that support for the Progress Party in Denmark increased when unemployment and the number of foreigners increased. He also found that the Progress Party benefited in public opinion polls after it had increased its vote in national elections and if a left government were in power.

Unfortunately, regional data on unemployment and the number of immigrants were unavailable for the Danish case, so I cannot conduct the same type of analysis as in Chapter 4. Based on Anderson's findings, there appears to be some relationship. However, in Figure 7.2 the percentage of foreigners and unemployment at the national level are compared with the vote for the radical right (combined vote of the DPP and Progress Party). Unemployment has actually been in decline in Denmark since 1993, so it has not been much of an issue in Danish politics. However, as noted earlier, the percentage of foreigners has been increasing, and many of the new arrivals are asylum seekers and refugees from outside Europe. This trend shows a fundamental change in immigration flows and has helped to fuel anti-immigrant rhetoric.

As with the other cases, unemployment and foreigners cannot provide a full explanation for the success of the radical right in Denmark. Although the percentage of foreigners has increased, it is still far below the 9% of foreigners in Austria and Germany. As with these cases, there are obviously other factors playing a role in the radical right's success.

Party Leadership

Mogens Glistrup's personality was clearly a driving force behind the early success of the Progress Party. Over time, however, Glistrup became a liability, as his pronouncements became more extreme, and his grip on the party loosened. Also, no other party wanted to work with the Progress Party. Although Pia Kjærsgaard doesn't have the same charismatic appeal

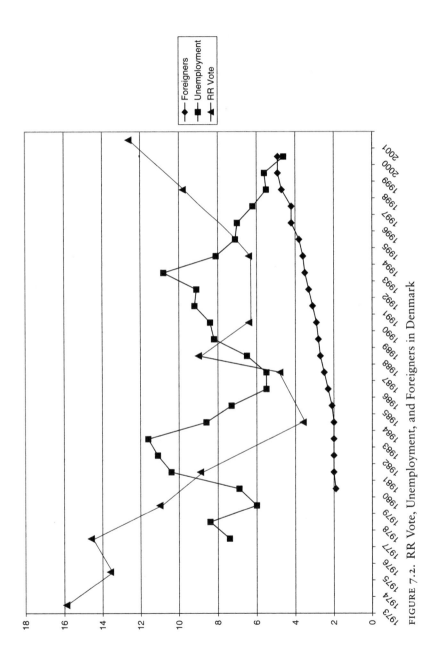

FIGURE 7.2. RR Vote, Unemployment, and Foreigners in Denmark

that Glistrup had when he began the Progress Party, she has been a very successful leader of the new party (DPP) that she founded.

Kjærsgaard has been characterized in the popular media as a "blonde elfin housewife and mother of two." The media paid a great deal of attention to Kjærsgaard in the run-up to the September 2000 vote on joining the "Euro zone." The referendum was defeated, which strengthened Kjærsgaard and others in the "no" camp. The immigration issue also helped Kjærsgaard in the run-up to the 2001 election. The party is clearly for tighter immigration control. In August 2001, the party purchased a full-page newspaper ad that listed nearly 5000 newly naturalized Danes, most of whom were from outside Europe. The ad criticized the government for allowing the naturalization of these "new Danes."

Kjærsgaard doesn't have the same level of appeal as does Jörg Haider in Austria, but she has managed to consolidate power in her party and is an effective campaigner. Other party leaders described her as being very effective with the media, and she is clearly responsible for the party's high level of visibility. Her leadership put the DPP in a position to work with the ruling parties after the 2001 election. In the next section, I discuss the role of strategic voting in that election.

7.3. PR AND STRATEGIC VOTING IN DENMARK

Thus far I have provided mainly a descriptive analysis of the radical right in Denmark. In this section, I explore the hypothesis that strategic voting has not suppressed the vote for the radical right in Denmark. As with the analysis in Chapter 6, I begin by describing the electoral system, then I describe factionalism and coalition strategies. The section concludes with an empirical analysis of strategic voting.

Electoral System

The electoral system in Denmark is a PR system with a few twists to make it complicated. Jørgen Elklit (1993) has argued, however, that the Danish electoral system is much "simpler than its reputation." The system is based on proportional representation, and three quarters of all seats are allocated by PR, with the remaining seats used as "adjustment seats" (Elklit 1993). There are 17 multi-member electoral districts, and voters get one vote and choose either a party or a candidate.

The Danish system gets complicated when one looks at the allocation of seats at the subnational level, but Elklit argues that the Danish system could be considered similar to the German electoral system, since they are both "primarily systems of national allocation and national proportionality among parties exceeding some electoral threshold" (Elklit 1993, 54). The electoral threshold in the Danish system is 2%, compared with 5% in the German system. Both the Danish and German systems allow voters to vote for a particular candidate, which serves to tie candidates to their constituency. However, the Danish system does not provide voters with the same incentives for strategic voting as the German system, since the threshold is lower, and voters only get one vote in the Danish system.

Factionalism

As noted earlier, the radical right in Denmark has had to deal with intraparty factionalism that ultimately led to the formation of the Danish People's Party. As Widfeldt notes, the split was between fundamentalists and pragmatists within the Progress Party. The fundamentalist faction, to which Glistrup belonged, advocated an "all or nothing" policy where compromises or broad agreements with the established parties were out of the question. The pragmatists, with Pia Kjærsgaard as a leading name, were more willing to negotiate with other parties, such as the Liberal Party, in order to achieve political results (Widfeldt 2000). Although this split eventually led to the formation of the DPP, the split actually gave a boost to Kjærsgaard and her defectors. Glistrup had become a liability with his jail sentence, and, once out of jail, he became an embarrassment for the pragmatists in the party. Kjaersgaard had a level of credibility that Glistrup lacked, and she was able to create a more unified party.

Coalition Strategies

Coalition strategies in Denmark are complicated by the fact that the country has had mainly minority governments (often formed by more than one party) since the early 1980s. Although coalition formation tends to be played up in the media prior to an election, voters have come to expect that a minority government will form, and the ruling parties will rely on different parties to find a majority for a particular piece of legislation. In a sense, the formation of minority governments in Denmark has had a similar effect on voters as the formation of great coalitions has had in Austria. Voters know that a coalition will form, even without a majority, so a party or coalition does not have to get a majority of the

TABLE 7.3. *Coalition Signals in Denmark Elections March 11 1998 and November 20 2001*

Date	Signal (from : to)	Source	Article*
Coalition Signals – Denmark 1997–1998			
March 24th	CD: Not SD/RL, but skeptic of LP/CPP as well	Party Leadership	Z1588757
April 25th	CrP: Not SD/RL, but neither LP candidate as prime minister	Party Leadership	Z1669659
May 10th	CD: Not LP/CPP	Party Leadership	Z1704959
June 29th	SPP: SD/RL	News Media	Z1838825
September 28th	DPP: LP/CPP (on certain conditions)	Party Convention	Z2143079
October 5th	DPP: LP/CPP (on certain conditions)	Party Convention	Z2168220
October 11th	SD: Not LP/CPP (either opposition or the prime minister post)	Party Leadership	Z2354116
October 17th	DPP: LP/CPP (on certain conditions)	Party Leadership	Z2351160
December 20th	LP: Not DPP	Party Member (but internal disagreement)	Z2546177
January 12th	RL: SD and not LP/CPP	Party Leadership	Z2598794
February 21st	UL and SPP: SD/RL; PP and DPP: LP/CPP	Party Leadership	Z2693357
March 2nd	SD: Not DPP or PP	Party Leadership	Z2715458
Coalition Signals – Denmark 2000–2001			
December 2nd	DPP: SD	Party Leadership (but internal disagreement)	Y0197064
December 4th	UL, SPP: RL not SD ("too identical to DPP")	Party Leadership	Y0200221
January 19th	RL: SD (on certain conditions)	Party Leadership	Y0377017
February 13th	LP/CPP: DPP	News Media	Y0473032
February 17th	LP: DPP	Party Leadership	Y0488394
March 16th	LP: DPP	Party Leadership	Y0599209
March 27th	LP/CPP: DPP	News Media	Y0638999
May 11th	CpP: LP/CPP	Party Member	Y0835112
June 24th	LP/CPP: DPP	Survey	Y0992337
August 19th	LP/CPP: DPP	News Media	Y1245027
August 26th	SD: SPP	Party Leadership	Y1268293
September 6th	CD: LP/CPP (on certain conditions)	Party Leadership	Y1309827
September 11th	CD: LP (on certain conditions)	Party Leadership	Y1328306

Date	Signal (from : to)	Source	Article*
September 16th	DPP: LP/CPP	Party Convention	Y1345635
September 17th	DPP: LP/CPP	Party Convention	Y1348119
September 22nd	CD: LP (on certain conditions)	Party Leadership	Y1381527
October 6th	LP/CPP: DPP	Party Leadership	Y1375734
October 16th	LP/CPP: DPP	Party Leadership	Y1477467
November 2nd	SPP: SD	Party Leadership	Y1674431
November 4th	LP: DPP	News Media	Y1683436
November 13th	SD: RL, SPP, UL	Party Leadership	Y1733137
November 17th	LP/CPP: CD, CpP, and DPP	Party Leadership	Y1769805

* Infomedia, http://www.polinfo.dk, article number references.
Source: Infomedia. http://www.polinfo.dk, 03/11/1997 to 03/11/1998 and 11/20/2000 to 11/20/2001. Keywords: "støtteparti" (supporting party), "koalition" (coalition), and "parlamentarisk grundlag" (parliamentary backing).

votes, just as the voters in Austria know that the two top parties will not get a majority.

As with the other cases, parties in Denmark often signal their coalition preferences prior to an election, as shown in Table 7.3. What is interesting from the 1998 election is that most often the parties were indicating with whom they would *not* go into coalition. The center parties in particular (CD and CrP) made moves long before the election to indicate which parties they would support, although these announcements were probably designed to gain policy concessions from possible coalition partners.

Over time, the parties in Denmark have tended to work with traditional coalition partners on the left and right. For example, the Liberal Party has tended to be in coalitions with the Conservative People's Party, and the Social Democrats have formed coalitions with the Socialist People's Party. The smaller center and extreme parties, such as the CD, CrP, and UL, were not necessarily guaranteed spots in a governing coalition. Table 7.3 indicates that it was mostly these smaller parties that were likely to indicate their coalition preferences, with the exception of the Liberal Party in 2001, which indicated its willingness to form a minority government supported by the DPP as early as February of that year. In general, for the larger mainstream parties, coalition signaling was not an important factor in the election.

The 2001 election brought the radical right into a working majority with the mainstream right. As in Austria, a right-wing Danish government was willing to work with the radical right. What is different from the Austrian case was the Liberal Party's willingness to declare its intention to govern with a coalition supported by the radical right prior to the election. As indicated in Table 7.3, during the 2001 election the LP indicated several times that it was willing to form a minority coalition government with the support of the Danish People's Party. This signaling is likely to have boosted support for the DPP by reducing strategic desertion of the party.

Data Analysis

To test strategic voting in Denmark, I have taken data from elections in which the radical right competed (1973–2001) at the district level. There are 17 electoral districts in Denmark, and there were 13 elections during this time period for an N (total number) of 221. As with the regression analyses in Chapter 6, the issue is whether voters are less likely to vote for a radical right party when the vote between the mainstream parties is close.

The first column in Table 7.4 is the combined vote of the Progress Party and the Danish People's Party. The relationship of this radical right vote to the absolute value of the mainstream party vote (combined vote of the Social Democrats and the Socialist People's Party on the left, and the Liberal Party and the Conservative People's Party on the right) is actually negative, indicating that as the difference between the mainstream parties *increases* the vote for the radical right *decreases*. This is the opposite of what we would expect in the presence of strategic voting and is therefore

TABLE 7.4. *Relationship of FP–DPP Vote with Difference in Mainstream Party Vote[1] (absolute value)*

	Pooled Data – Electoral District Level		
	Radical Right Vote 1973–2001	Radical Right Vote 1981–2001	Danish People's Party Vote 1998–2001
Constant	11.54**	9.10**	9.43**
	(1.47)	(1.29)	(2.44)
[Right-Left]	−0.117**	−0.094**	0.109
	(0.042)	(0.037)	(0.149)
N	204	136	34

** Indicates significant at .05 level of confidence.

consistent with my hypothesis. We would expect voters to be more likely to vote for the radical right as the difference between the two parties increases. This result is similar to those found in the case of Germany in 1969 and the Austrian case in general.

I also have broken down the data into two different samples. The first sample (center column, Table 7.4) includes data on the radical right since 1981, to exclude the period when the Progress Party first crashed onto the scene. The results in this case are similar to the original regression. In the second sample (right column, Table 7.4), I examine results only for the Danish People's Party. In this case, the result is positive, but the results are not significantly different from zero. None of these cases provides support for strategic voting.

7.4. CONCLUSION

The results in Denmark compare to those of the Austrian case. The Danish results indicate that strategic voting is less likely in PR systems in which the mainstream parties/coalitions regularly fail to get a majority of the vote. Voters may not feel the need to strategically desert a small party in these circumstances, since their party will win seats and is not likely to have a negative effect on their coalition preferences. These findings support my hypothesis that radical right parties are more likely to be successful in the absence of strategic voting. Institutional factors such as electoral rules, combined with party strategy (or lack thereof), do play a role in the success of the radical right and can explain large variations in support for similar parties, by similar electorates, across countries.

The radical right's success in Denmark is likely to continue, unless the mainstream parties are willing to work together to discourage voters from supporting the Danish People's Party, as in the French case. Economic upheaval and inflows of foreigners will continue to provide a basis for the radical right's appeal. The survival of these RR parties lies not only in the radical right's strategies but also in the strategies and choices made by the mainstream parties. In the next chapter, I review the findings from the previous chapters and explore the implications of my analysis.

8

Conclusion

8.1. THE PUZZLE REVISITED

Given that all four countries face similar socioeconomic conditions, why is the radical right more successful at winning votes in Denmark, France, and Austria than in Germany? Why does the radical right gain more seats in Denmark and Austria than in France? This book has focused on the puzzle that is presented by the difference in the level of success of radical right parties. The results of this analysis imply that electoral rules and party systems play a crucial role in the development of new parties. Electoral results can be difficult to understand unless these rules and the strategies that parties pursue are included in the analysis. In general, the comparative study of political parties can benefit from an understanding of the strategies that voters and parties use to gain particular outcomes. Changes in the rules of the game can have a dramatic impact on party development and electoral success. To conclude the analysis, I summarize the findings of the previous chapters, discuss the implications of those findings, and identify areas for future research.

This analysis has emphasized the importance of electoral institutions, factionalism, and party strategy in explaining the difference in levels of success of radical right parties in Western Europe. In Chapter 1, I presented my main argument: that radical right parties will have difficulty attracting voters and winning seats in electoral systems that encourage strategic voting and/or strategic coordination by the mainstream parties. I described the comparative literature on the radical right, the basis of support for the parties in each country, and my research design. To maximize the system-level variables that can be controlled across cases, I used a "most similar systems" design. I also confirmed that a puzzle exists in levels of electoral support for the radical right, by providing evidence that the radical right parties have similar levels of support in surveys and European elections.

The main argument of Chapter 2 is that the radical right parties can be classified in the same category due to their nationalism and the positions they take on issues such as immigration and the economy. I began by comparing different authors' definitions of extreme or radical right parties and developed my own description of a radical right party. I then described the radical right parties in France, Germany, and Austria and their histories, including the factionalism that each party has experienced. Despite differences in their historical development during the 1980s and 1990s, a review of party materials showed that the parties tend toward nationalism and have taken very similar positions on issues such as immigration and the European Union.

The main argument in Chapter 3 is that *differences in who votes for the radical right cannot explain the difference in its level of success.* It is difficult to show systematically that differences in the level of success of radical right parties are caused by differences in the types of voters they attract. I argue that what is remarkable about radical right parties in Western Europe is not the difference in their electorates, but the similarities, no matter their level of electoral success. To support my argument, I compared the electorates of radical right parties in France, Germany, and Austria during the 1980s and 1990s. I placed the argument within the context of traditional cleavages, their effect on voting behavior, and the decline in the influence of these cleavages.

I used survey data in Chapter 3 to determine if there were differences in the types of respondents who voted for the radical right. The survey data demonstrated that the constituencies of the radical right parties were actually becoming more similar over time. If the social structures of the constituencies are becoming similar, differences in those structures cannot explain the differences in the percentage of the vote received by radical right parties. I demonstrated that there are few differences in the types of social groups who vote for the radical right across countries, when traditional cleavages and changes in the structure of the vote over time are taken into account.

The analysis in Chapter 4 uses methods similar to those of authors such as Kitschelt (1995), Betz (1994), and Swank and Betz (1995). I extend the types of analyses used by these authors in several ways: using data at the regional, rather than national level; using longer time periods; and

comparing the data results for the radical right with those of the mainstream parties. I used regression analysis to determine if a relationship
existed between the vote for the radical right, immigration, and unemployment. I found that this analysis was not sufficient to explain the difference
in the vote for the radical right parties. A relationship existed between
these variables in France and Austria, but not in Germany, despite the
fact that Germany has levels of unemployment and immigration similar
to the other cases.

The approach taken in Chapter 3 focused on voter behavior, without
taking into account the impact of exogenous factors such as institutions.
The regression analysis in Chapter 4 examined the role of exogenous
factors such as immigration and unemployment, thus providing an incentive for voters. This approach, however, could not explain why the presence of these factors did not have an effect on the radical right vote in
Germany.

In Chapter 5, I developed a model to support my hypothesis that
electoral institutions, factionalism, and strategic voting can explain the
difference in the vote for the radical right. Cox's theories on electoral
institutions are the basis for my analysis of strategic voting and strategic
coordination by parties. In Chapter 6, I used case studies and regression
analysis to provide evidence that the different electoral rules in France,
Germany, and Austria have produced different strategies and incentives
for parties and voters. Voters are less likely to vote for the radical right
in Germany because of strategic voting. The radical right in France is less
likely to win seats due to strategic coordination by the mainstream parties.
In Austria, great coalition governments and a proportional representation
(PR) system provide a difficult environment for strategic voting.

To determine if the model I have developed made sense in a broader
context, I chose Denmark as an additional test case. Denmark has a pure
PR system (unlike France and Germany), and the mainstream parties have
alternated in power (unlike Austria). The main difference between Denmark and the other cases in this book is the predominance of minority
governments. The impact of minority government coalition formation on
voter expectations, however, displays similar dynamics as the formation
of great coalition governments in Austria. In both cases, voters have little
reason to believe they need to vote strategically for a coalition. The statistical analysis indicates, as in the Austrian case, that strategic voting does
not influence the vote for the radical right in Denmark.

My findings do not necessarily dispute what other authors have found.
What I do provide is a more nuanced understanding of the role of party

strategy and strategic voting in the success of the radical right. It is not only the strategy of the radical right but also the structure of the electoral system and coalition strategy that influence strategic voting. However, strategic voting by itself cannot explain the success of the radical right. Strategic voting influences a party's ability to attract a particular constituency, but as Kitschelt finds (1995), a party must use the right appeal to attract voters. The right economic and social conditions also must be in place for a radical right party to succeed. Strategic voting comes into play when these other conditions are in place, and the absence of strategic voting can thus be thought of as a necessary but not sufficient condition for radical right success.

8.2. IMPLICATIONS

The main point of this study is that institutions determine the "rules of the game" and need to be taken into account when comparing party systems and the differences in the level of success of particular parties in different countries. The results of this analysis imply that electoral rules and party systems play an important role in the development and success of new parties. Voters and parties are not automatons that respond reflexively to societal conditions; instead, they pursue strategies to achieve their goals. Strategies that parties pursue are difficult to understand unless these rules and party systems are included in the analysis. In general, the comparative study of political parties can benefit from the consideration of institutions.

Changes in the rules of the game can have a dramatic impact on party development and electoral success. This is highlighted by the impact of the change of electoral rules in France in 1986. In that election, the National Front (FN) was able to win seats because a proportional representation system was used. When the system was returned to the single-member dual-ballot (SMDB) system, the FN was unable to win seats. Clearly, electoral institutions played a defining role in this case.

The French case also highlights the role of cooperation between mainstream parties, which successfully kept the radical right from winning seats. The mainstream right in France was willing to follow a moral consensus with the "Republican Front" strategy, but this consensus broke down when the mainstream right found that the strategy was hurting the right's electoral chances. The mainstream right did, however, pursue a strategy of excluding the radical right, to the point of sanctioning regional politicians who worked with the FN. The mainstream right paid the price in the short term, but in the long term the strategy was successful.

In the cases I have examined, the impact of institutions has kept the German National Democratic Party (NPD) and *Republikaner* from winning seats in the German *Bundestag* and kept the French National Front from winning more than one seat in the legislature, with the exception of the 1986 election described earlier. The electoral systems in Germany and France have provided the mainstream parties with a means to maintain their control of the legislature, and one would expect that they would avoid changes to these rules that might help to change the balance of power.

In the German case, there are still possibilities for success of the radical right at the *Land* level. In the 2004 election in Saxony, the NPD won 9.2% of the vote and 12 seats. The NPD has been developing a following in East Germany, attracting young, unemployed men in particular. It seems unlikely that the NPD will be able to translate this success into winning 5% of the national vote and seats at the national level, but it could use Saxony as a base to try to win 3 seats in the *Bundestag*, which would allow the party representation at the national level. However, previous success by the Republikaner at the *Land* level in Baden-Württemburg did not translate into seats at the national level. It remains to be seen if the NPD can avoid the factionalism that has hurt other parties and overcome the perception that the vote in Saxony was mainly a protest of reforms proposed by the Schröder government.

The Austrian and Danish cases suggest that PR systems may make it difficult for larger parties to keep small parties from gaining vote shares. However, the Freedom Party (FPÖ) could not have been successful without the change in economic conditions and immigration, and the long-term presence of the great coalition that appears to have sparked its success. The Danish People's Party (DPP) may not have been as successful without the indication from the conservatives that DPP support would be accepted by a minority government. It is the combination of favorable conditions, including socioeconomic factors and electoral institutions, that create an environment in which the radical right can achieve electoral success.

This analysis also implies that time is an important consideration when studying differences in parties' success. A party's constituency can change with time, and an analysis that only considers a short time period may come to false conclusions. Other factors, such as economic conditions, also change with time, and a party's ability to adapt to such changes can have an impact on its success.

The examination of socioeconomic factors adds to a comparative analysis by providing an understanding of the relationship between increases and decreases in prosperity and the level of success of a particular party. Increases in unemployment did have an impact on the vote for the radical right, in countries where it was successful. This analysis also looked specifically at the impact of immigrants in a region. The combination of economic decline, and the presence of immigrants who are perceived to exacerbate that decline, can have an impact on a party's success.

Despite the relationships found in this analysis, only time will tell if the radical right will continue to be dependent on the socioeconomic situation in a country to expand its appeal. For the mainstream parties, trying to address issues related to immigration will not make the radical right disappear. This is a lesson that has certainly been learned in France. Despite the government's attempts to control immigration, the FN continued to perform well in both local and national elections, mainly at the expense of the conservative parties.

8.3. FURTHER RESEARCH

One of the first steps for further research would be to add more countries to the analysis. This book is limited to a comparison of four countries, but the same methods can be used to study any country facing similar background conditions. Adding countries to the analysis may help to confirm the role of institutions, not only in the vote for the radical right but also in the vote for other small parties that attempt to compete in different electoral systems.

The issue of institutional design also is important. The Austrian case raises the question of why the mainstream parties have not tried to change the rules in their favor. The mainstream parties can certainly make strategic calculations to determine which electoral rules could work in their favor, as they did in the French case when abandoning PR. However, there are tradeoffs in changing the rules that must be a part of the equation. Developing a model that could explain the incentives for changing the electoral rules would be a useful addition to a comparative analysis.

Another part of electoral institutions not addressed in this book is party finance. The rules that govern a party's ability to raise funds, as well as funds that come from the state, can be manipulated in favor of established parties. Comparing the nature of party finance in each country may provide additional insight into the success of small parties.

Future research can benefit from the type of analyses developed in this book. Institutional structures provide a framework that can determine electoral incentives for voters and parties. With this framework, it is possible to develop testable hypotheses about the behavior of parties and voters and to compare the outcomes across countries. This type of approach is useful for the study of a variety of questions related to parties and party systems.

The rise of radical right parties in the 1980s and 1990s is a symptom of political change that is occurring across Western Europe. The radical right parties have presented the mainstream parties with a challenge. The particular ways in which this challenge is met will continue to be shaped by the institutions in each country, despite the social similarities of those who follow radical right appeals and the ideological similarities of those appeals themselves.

References

Algazy, Joseph. 1989. *L'Extrême-Droite en France de 1965 a 1984*. Paris: L'Harmattan.

Allport, G. W. 1954. *The Nature of Prejudice*. New York: Doubleday Books.

Alvarez, Michael and Jonathan Nagler. 2000. "A New Approach for Modelling Strategic Voting in Multiparty Elections." *British Journal of Political Science* 30:57–75.

Anderson, Christopher J. 1996. "Economics, Politics and Foreigners: Populist Party Support in Denmark and Norway." *Electoral Studies* 15:497–511.

Andersen, Jørgen Goul and Tor Bjørklund. 2000. "Radical Right-Wing Populism in Scandinavia: From Tax Revolt to Neo-Liberalism and Xenophobia," in *The Politics of the Extreme Right: From the Margins to the Mainstream*, ed. Paul Hainsworth. New York: Pinter.

Andersen, Uwe and Wichard Woyke. 1995. *Handwörterbuch des Politischen Systems der Bundesrepublik Deutschland*, 2. auflage. Opladen, Germany: Leske und Budrich.

Assheuer, T. and H. Sarkowicz. 1992. *Rechtsradikale in Deutschland: Die Alte und die Neue Rechte*. Munich: Beck.

Atkinson, Graeme. 1993. "Germany: Nationalism, Nazism and Violence," in *Racist Violence in Europe*, ed. Tore Björgo and Rob Witte. London: Macmillan.

Baguenard, Jacques. 1986. *La France Electorale*. Paris: Presses Universitaires de France.

Bailer-Galanda, Brigitte and Wolfgang Neugebauer. 1997. *Haider und die "Freiheitlichen" in Österreich*. Berlin: Elefanten Press.

Balibar, Etienne. 1991. "Es Gibt Keinen Staat in Europe: Racism and Politics in Europe Today." *New Left Review* 186:5–19.

Bawn, Kathleen. 1993. "The Logic of Institutional Preferences: German Electoral Law as a Social Choice Outcome." *American Journal of Political Science* 37:965–989.

————. 1998. "Voter Responses to Electoral Complexity: Ticket Splitting, Rational Voters and Representation in the Federal Republic of Germany." Unpublished mss.

Beck, Nathaniel and Jonathan N. Katz. 1995. "What to Do (and Not to Do) with Time-Series Cross-Section Data." *American Political Science Review* 89:634–647.

Bell, D. 1976. "The Extreme Right in France," in *Social and Political Movements in Western Europe*, ed. M. Kolinsky and W. E. Paterson. London: Croom Helm.

Betz, Hans-Georg. 1991. *Postmodern Politics in Germany: The Politics of Resentment*. New York: St. Martin's Press.

————. 1994. *Radical Right Wing Populism in Western Europe*. New York: St. Martin's Press.

————. 1997. "Globalisierung und Neopopulismus." Unpublished mss. Spring.

Betz, Hans-Georg and Markus Crepaz. 1997. "Postindustrial Cleavages and Electoral Change in an Advanced Capitalist Democracy: The Austrian Case." Unpublished mss. Spring.

Bille, Lars. 2001. Interview by author, Copenhagen, Denmark, August 21.

Biorcio, R. 1993. "The Rebirth of Populism in Italy and France." *Telos* 90 (Winter):43–56.

Birthler, Marianne. 1993. *Deutschland vor der Wahl*. Göttingen: Lamuv.

Blais, André, Richard Nadeau, Elisabeth Gidengil, and Neil Nevitte. 2001. "Measuring Strategic Voting in Multiparty Plurality Elections." *Electoral Studies* 20:343–352.

Blinkhorn, M. 1990. *Fascists and Conservatives: The Radical Right and the Establishment in Twentieth Century Europe*. London: Unwin Hyman.

Borre, Ole and Jørgen Goul Andersen. 1997. *Voting and Political Attitudes in Denmark*. Aarhus, Denmark: Aarhus University Press.

Braunthal, Gerard. 1996. *Parties and Politics in Modern Germany*. Boulder, Colorado: Westview Press.

Brechon, Pierre and Subrata Kumar Mitra. 1993. "The National Front in France: The Emergence of an Extreme Right Protest Movement." *Comparative Politics* 25 (October):63–82.

Brubaker, Rogers. 1992. *Citizenship and Nationhood in France and Germany*. Cambridge, Massachusetts: Harvard University Press.

————. ed. 1989. *Immigration and the Politics of Citizenship in Europe and North America*. New York: University Press of America.

Brustein, William. 1996. *The Logic of Evil*. New Haven: Yale University Press.

Caciagli, Mario. 1988. "The Movimento Sociale Italiano-Destra Nazionale and Neo-Fascism in Italy." *West European Politics* 11 (April):19–33.

Castles, Stephen. 1995. "How Nation-States Respond to Immigration and Ethnic Diversity." *New Community* 21 (3):293–308.

Castles, Stephen, with Heather Booth and Tina Wallace. 1984. *Here for Good: Western Europe's New Ethnic Minorities*. New South Wales, Australia: Pluto Press.

Cerny, Karl H. 1990. "The Campaign and the 1987 Election Outcome," in *Germany at the Polls: The Bundestag Elections of the 1980s*, ed. Karl H. Cerny. Durham, North Carolina: Duke University Press.

Chapin, Wesley D. 1997. "Explaining the Electoral Success of the New Right: The German Case." *West European Politics* 20:53–73.

Chebel d'Appollonia, Ariane. 1988. *L'Extrême-Droite en France: De Maurras à Le Pen.* Bruxelles: Editions Complexe.

Cheles, Luciano, Ronnie Ferguson, and Michalina Vaughan. 1995. *The Far Right in Western and Eastern Europe.* New York: Longman.

Chiarini, Roberto. 1991. "The 'Movimento Sociale Italiano': A Historical Profile," in *Neo-Fascism in Europe,* ed. Luciano Cheles, Ronnie Ferguson, and Michalina Vaughan, 19–42. Essex, England: Longman Group.

Childs, David. 1991. "The Far Right in Germany since 1945," in *Neo-Fascism in Europe,* ed. Luciano Cheles, Ronnie Ferguson, and Michalina Vaughan, 66–85. Essex, England: Longman Group.

Chladek, Josef. 1997. "Sonntagsfrage: Wenn am Kommenden Sonntag NR-Wahlen Wären, wem Würden Sie dann Ihre Stimme Geben?" *Profil Online.* Available at http://www.profil.at/cgi-bin/politik/index.html. Accessed January 18, 1999.

Cole, Alistair, ed. 1990. *French Political Parties in Transition.* Brookfield, Vermont: Dartmouth Publishing.

Conradt, David P. 1996. *The German Polity,* 6th ed. White Plains, New York: Longman.

Conradt, David P., Gerald R. Kleinfeld, George K. Romoser, and Christian Søe. 1995. *Germany's New Politics: Parties and Issues in the 1990s.* Providence, Rhode Island: Berghahn Books.

Cornelius, Wayne A., Philip L. Martin, and James F. Hollifield, eds. 1994. *Controlling Immigration: A Global Perspective.* Stanford: Stanford University Press.

Cox, Gary. 1997. *Making Votes Count: Strategic Coordination in the World's Electoral Systems.* Cambridge: Cambridge University Press.

Dachs, Herbert. 1992. *Parteien und Wahlen in Österreichs Bundesländern 1945–1991.* Munchen: R. Oldenbourg Verlag.

Dalton, J. Russell. 1993. *The New Germany Votes: Unification and the Creation of a German Party System.* Providence, Rhode Island: Berg.

———. 1996. *Citizen Politics: Public Opinion and Political Parties in Advanced Western Democracies,* 2nd ed. Chatham, New Jersey: Chatham House Publishers.

DeClair, Edward G. 1999. *Politics on the Fringe: The People, Policies and Organization of the French National Front.* Durham, North Carolina: Duke University Press.

Denardo, James. 1985. *Power in Numbers: The Political Strategy of Protest and Rebellion.* Princeton, New Jersey: Princeton University Press.

Dokumentationsarchiv des Österreichischen Widerstandes. 1994. *Handbuch des Österreichischen Rechtsextremismus.* Wien: Deuticke.

Dowding, Keith and Desmond King, eds. 1995. *Preferences, Institutions, and Rational Choice.* New York: Oxford University Press.

Downs, Anthony. 1957. *An Economic Theory of Democracy.* New York: Harper & Brothers.

Dragnich, Alex and Jorgen S. Rasmussen, eds. 1986. *Major European Governments.* Pacific Grove, California: Brooks/Cole.

Duprat, François. 1990. *Les Mouvements d'Extrême Droite en Europe de l'Ouest:*
Actes de Colloque d'Anvers (29 Mars 1990). Brussels: VUB Press.

Durand, Géraud. 1996. *Enquête au Cœur du Front National.* Paris: Jacques
Grancher.

Duverger, Maurice. 1954. *Political Parties.* New York: Wiley.

Eatwell, Roger. 1995. "How to Revise History (and Influence People?), Neo-
Fascist Style," in *The Far Right in Western and Eastern Europe,* ed. Luciano
Cheles, Ronnie Ferguson, and Michalina Vaughan. New York: Longman.

———. 2000. "The Extreme-Right and British Exceptionalism: The Primacy of
Politics," in *The Politics of the Extreme Right: From the Margins to the Mainstream,* ed. Paul Hainsworth. New York: Pinter.

Edye, Dave. 1987. *Immigrant Labour and Government Policy: The Cases of the*
Federal Republic of Germany and France. Aldershot, England: Gower Publishing Company Ltd.

Eilfort, Michael. 1992. "Sind Nichtwähler auch Wähler?" in *Protestwähler und*
Wahlverweigerer, ed. Karl Starzacher, Konrad Schacht, Bernd Friedrich, and
Thomas Leif. Köln: Bund-Verlag.

Elklit, Jørgen. 1993. "Simpler than Its Reputation: The Electoral System in
Denmark since 1920." *Electoral Studies* 12:41–57.

Ely, John. 1993. "The 'Black-Brown Hazelnut' in a Bigger Germany: The Rise
of a Radical Right as a Structural Feature," in *From Bundesrepublik to*
Deutschland: German Politics after Unification, ed. Michael G. Huelshoff,
Andrei S. Markovits, and Simon Reich. Ann Arbor: University of Michigan
Press.

———. 1989. "Republicans: Neo-Nazis or the Black-Brown Hazelnut? Recent
Successes of the Radical Right in West Germany." *German Politics and Society*
18 (Fall):1–17.

Esser, Hartmut and Hermann Korte. 1985. "Federal Republic of Germany," in
European Immigration Policy, ed. Tomas Hammar. Cambridge: Cambridge
University Press.

Falter, Jürgen. 1994. *Wer Wählt Rechts?* Munich: Beck.

Falter, Jürgen and Siegfried Schumann. 1988. "Affinity towards Right-Wing
Extremism in Western Europe." *West European Politics* 11 (April):96–113.

Fennema, Meindert. 1996. *Some Theoretical Problems and Issues in Comparison*
of Anti-Immigrants Parties in Western Europe. Barcelona: Institut de Ciencias
Politiques i Socials.

Fink, Willibald. 1969. *Die NPD bei der Bayerischen Landtagswahl 1966.* Wien:
Olzog.

Fisher, Stephen L. 1973. "The Wasted Vote Thesis: West German Evidence." *Comparative Politics* 5:293–299.

Fisichella, Domenico. 1984. "The Double Ballot-System as a Weapon against Anti-
System Parties," in *Choosing and Electoral System: Issues and Alternatives,* ed.
Arend Lijphart and Bernard Grofman. New York: Praeger.

Franklin, Mark, Tom Mackie, and Henry Valen. 1992. *Electoral Change:*
Responses to Evolving Social and Attitudinal Structures in Western Countries.
New York: Cambridge University Press.

Freeman, Gary P. 1979. *Immigrant Labor and Racial Conflict in Industrial Societies.* Princeton, New Jersey: Princeton University Press, 1979.

———. 2001. "Client Politics or Populism? Immigration Reform in the United States" pp. 65–96 in *Controlling a New Migration World*, ed. Virginie Guiraudon and Christian Joppke. London and New York: Routledge.

———. 1994. "Modes of Immigration Politics in the Receiving States." Paper presented at the Conference on Immigration into Western Societies, Charleston, South Carolina, May 13–14.

Friedrich, Robert J. 1982. "In Defense of Multiplicative Terms in Multiple Regression Equations." *American Journal of Political Science* 26 (November):797–833.

Fullbrook, Mary. 1994. "The Threat of the Radical Right in Germany." *Patterns of Prejudice* 28 (3–4):57–66.

Gallagher, Michael, Michael Laver, and Peter Mair. 1992. *Representative Government in Western Europe*. New York: McGraw-Hill.

Garrett, Geoffrey and Peter Lange. 1991. "Political Responses to Interdependence: What's 'Left' for the Left?" *International Organization* 45 (Autumn):539–564.

Geddes, Barbara. 1990. "How the Cases You Choose Affect the Answers You Get: Selection Bias in Comparative Politics," in *Political Analysis*, vol. 2, ed. James A. Stimson. Ann Arbor: University of Michigan Press.

Gehmacher, Ernst and Christian Haerpfer. 1989. "Voting Behavior and the Party System," in *The Austrian Party System*, ed. Anton Pelinka and Fritz Plasser. Boulder, Colorado: Westview Press.

Gellner, Ernest. 1983. *Nations and Nationalism*. Ithaca, New York: Cornell University Press.

German Federal Ministry of the Interior. 1993. *Survey of the Policy and Law Concerning Foreigners in the Federal Republic of Germany*. Bonn: Federal Ministry of the Interior, July.

Gibbons, Robert. 1992. *Game Theory for Applied Economists*. Princeton, New Jersey: Princeton University Press.

Gijsels, Hugo, et al. 1988. *Les Barbares: Les Immigres et le Racisme dans la Politique Belge*. Brussels: EPO/Celsius.

Givens, Terri E. 2004. "The Radical Right Gender Gap." *Comparative Political Studies*, 37:30–54.

Golden, Miriam A. 1997. *Heroic Defeats*. Cambridge: Cambridge University Press.

Greenwood, Michael J. and John M. McDowell. 1986. "The Factor Market Consequences of U.S. Immigration." *Journal of Economic Literature* 24 (December):1738–1772.

Gruber, Wolfgang. 1994. *Die Nationalratswahlkämpfe der SPÖ von 1970–1990*. Vienna: Diplomarbeit, Universität Wien.

Haider, Jörg. 1993. *Die Freiheit, die Ich Meine*. Frankfurt/Main: Ullstein.

Hainsworth, Paul, ed. 1992. *The Extreme Right in Europe and the USA*. London: Pinter.

———. 2000. *The Politics of the Extreme Right: From the Margins to the Mainstream*. London: Pinter.

Hargreaves, Alec. 1995. *Immigration, "Race" and Ethnicity in Contemporary France*. London: Routledge.

Hargreaves, Alec and Catherine Wihtol de Wenden. 1993. "The Political Participation of Ethnic Minorities in Europe: A Framework for Analysis," *New Community* 20 (1):1–8.

Heitmeyer, Wilhelm. 1993. "Hostility and Violence towards Foreigners in Germany," in *Racist Violence in Europe*, ed. Tore Björgo and Rob Witte. London: Macmillan.

Hennig, Eike. 1991. *Die Republikaner im Schatten Deutschlands: Zur Organisation der Mentalen Provinz: Eine Studie*. Frankfurt/Main: Suhrkamp.

Herbert, Ulrich. 1990. *A History of Foreign Labor in Germany, 1880–1980*. Ann Arbor: University of Michigan Press.

Hermansson, Magnus. 2001. "The Danish People's Party: Streamlined Right-Wing Gains Influence in Danish Politics." *Europe in the World 2001/2002: DaneViews*. Available at http://www.journalism.fcj.hvu.nl/Europe/kvdpp.html. Accessed May 8, 2002.

Hermens, Ferdinand A. 1984. "Representation and Proportional Representation," in *Choosing and Electoral System: Issues and Alternatives*, ed. Arend Lijphart and Bernard Grofman. New York: Praeger.

Hollifield, James Frank. 1992. *Immigrants, Markets and States: The Political Economy of Postwar Europe*. Cambridge, Massachusetts: Harvard University Press.

———. 1994. "Immigration and Republicanism in France: The Hidden Consensus," in *Controlling Immigration: A Global Perspective*, ed. Wayne A. Cornelius, Philip L. Martin, and James F. Hollifield. Stanford: Stanford University Press.

Hoskin, Marilyn. 1991. *New Immigrants and Democratic Society: Minority Integration in Western Democracies*. New York: Praeger.

Hoskin, Marilyn and Roy C. Fitzgerald. 1989. "German Immigration Policy and Politics," in *The Gatekeepers: Comparative Immigration Policy*, ed. Michael C. LeMay. New York: Praeger.

Huber, John and Ronald Inglehart. 1995. "Expert Interpretations of Party Space and Party Locations in 42 Societies." *Party Politics* 1 (January):73–111.

Hug, Simon. 2001. *Altering Party Systems: Strategic Behavior and the Emergence of New Political Parties in Western Democracies*. Ann Arbor: University of Michigan Press.

———. 1995. "A Puzzling Case: The Dutch Green Party in the Light of Theories on the Formation of New Political Parties." Unpublished mss. Université de Genève, February.

Husbands, Christopher T. 1981. "Contemporary Right-Wing Extremism in Western European Democracies: A Review Article." *European Journal of Political Research* 9:75–99.

Ignazi, Piero. 1992. "The Silent Counter-revolution: Hypotheses on the Emergence of Extreme Right-Wing Parties in Europe." *European Journal of Political Research* 22:101–121.

———. 1996. "The Crisis of Parties and the Rise of New Political Parties." *Party Politics* 2 (October):549–566.

Ignazi, Piero and Colette Ysmal. 1992. "New and Old Extreme Right Parties: The French National Front and the Italian Movimento Sociale." *European Journal of Political Research* 22:101–121.

Ignazi, Piero and Pascal Perrineau. 2002. "The Extreme Right in the June 1999 European Elections," in *Europe at the Polls: The European Elections of 1999*, ed. Pascal Perrineau, Gerard Grunberg, and Colette Ysmal. New York: Palgrave.

Inglehart, Ronald. 1990. *Culture Shift in Advanced Industrial Society*. Princeton, NJ: Princeton University Press.

Jaccard, James, Robert Turrisi, Choi K. Wan. 1990. *Interaction Effects in Multiple Regression*. Newbury Park, California: Sage Publications.

Jackman, Robert and Karin Volpert. 1996. "Conditions Favoring Parties of the Extreme Right in Western Europe." *British Journal of Political Science* 26:501–521.

Jaschke, Hans-Gerd. 1994. *Rechtsextremismus und Fremdenfeinlichkeit: Begriffe, Positionen, Praxisfelder*. Opladen, Germany: Westdeutscher Verlag.

Jesse, Eckhard. 1988. "Split-Voting in the Federal Republic of Germany: An Analysis of the Federal Elections from 1953 to 1987." *Electoral Studies* 7:109–124.

Kaase, Max. 1996. "Looking Ahead: Politics in Germany after the 1994 Bundestag Election," in *Germans Divided: The 1994 Bundestag Elections and the Evolution of the German Party System*, ed. Russell J. Dalton. Washington, D.C.: Berg.

Kiewiet, D. Roderick. 1983. *Macroeconomics and Micropolitics*. Chicago: University of Chicago Press.

King, Gary. 1997. *A Solution to the Ecological Inference Problem*. Princeton, New Jersey: Princeton University Press.

Kitschelt, Herbert. 1995. *The Radical Right in Western Europe*. Ann Arbor: University of Michigan Press.

Knapp, Andrew. 1994. *Gaullism since de Gaulle*. Brookfield, Vermont: Dartmouth Publishing.

Knight, Robert. 1992. "Haider, the Freedom Party and the Extreme Right in Austria." *Parliamentary Affairs* 45:285–299.

Kolinsky, Eva. 1992. "A Future for Right Extremism in Germany?" in *The Extreme Right in Europe and the USA*, ed. Paul Hainsworth. London: Pinter.

Kramer, Gerald. 1971. "The Ecological Fallacy Revisited: Aggregate-Versus Individual-Level Findings on Economics and Elections and Sociotropic Voting." *American Political Science Review* 65:131–143.

Kriesi, Hanspieter. 1995. "Movements of the Left, Movements of the Right. Putting the Mobilization of Two New Types of Social Movements into Political Contexts." Paper presented at the Conference on the Politics and Political Economy of Contemporary Capitalism, Berlin, Humboldt University, May 26–27.

Kuechler, Manfred. 1996. "Deutschland den Deutschen? Migration and Naturalization in the 1994 Campaign and Beyond," in *Germans Divided: The 1994 Bundestag Elections and the Evolution of the German Party System*, ed. Russell J. Dalton. Washington, D.C.: Berg.

———. 1995. "Xenophobie im Internationalen Vergleich," in *Rechtsextremismus*, ed. Jürgen W. Falter and Hans-Gerd Jaschke. *PVS-Sonderheft* (September [journal special issue]).

Lancelot, Alain. 1968. *L'Abstentionnisme Electoral en France*. Paris: Armand Colin.

Lauber, Volkmar, ed. 1996. *Contemporary Austrian Politics*. Boulder, Colorado: Westview Press.

Layton-Henry, Zig, ed. 1990. *The Political Rights of Migrant Workers in Western Europe*. London: Sage Publications.

Lewis-Beck, Michael S. 1988. *Economics and Elections: The Major Western Democracies.* Ann Arbor: University of Michigan Press.

———. 2000. *How France Votes.* New York: Chatham House Publishers.

Lewis-Beck, Michael S. and Glenn E. Mitchell, II. 1993. "French Electoral Theory: The National Front Test." *Electoral Studies* 12:112–127.

Lewis, Rand. 1991. *A Nazi Legacy: Right-Wing Extremism in Postwar Germany.* New York: Praeger.

Lijphart, Arend. 1994. *Electoral Systems and Party Systems: A Study of Twenty-Seven Democracies, 1945–1990.* New York: Oxford University Press.

Lijphart, Arend and Bernard Grofman, eds. 1984. *Choosing an Electoral System: Issues and Alternatives.* New York: Praeger.

Lipset, S. M. and Stein Rokkan. 1967. "Cleavage Structures, Party Systems and Voter Alignments: An Introduction" in *Party Systems and Voter Alignments,* ed. Seymour Martin Lipset and Stein Rokkan, 1–64. New York: The Free Press.

Lubbers, Marcel, Mérove Gijsberts, and Peer Scheepers. 2002. "Extreme Right-Wing Voting in Western Europe." *European Journal of Political Research* 41:345–378.

Mackie, Thomas and Richard Rose. 1991. *The International Almanac of Electoral History.* London: Macmillan.

Mair, Peter, ed. 1990. *The West European Party System.* New York: Oxford University Press.

Maor, Moshe. 1998. *Parties, Conflicts and Coalitions in Western Europe: Organisational Determinants of Coalition Bargaining.* New York: Routledge.

Marcus, Jonathan. 1995. *The National Front and French Politics.* New York: New York University Press.

Markus, Gregory. 1988. "The Impact of Personal and National Economic Conditions on the Presidential Vote: A Pooled Cross-sectional Analysis." *American Journal of Political Science* 32:137–154.

Martin, Philip L. 1994. "Germany, Reluctant Land of Immigration," in *Controlling Immigration: A Global Perspective,* ed. Wayne A. Cornelius, Philip L. Martin, and James F. Hollifield. Stanford: Stanford University Press.

Martin, Pierre. 1996. "Le Vote Le Pen." *Notes de la Fondation Saint-Simon* 84: Octobre-Novembre.

Mayer, Nonna. 2002. *Ces Français Qui Votent Le Pen.* Paris: Flammarion.

———. 1989. "Le Vote FN de Passy à Barbès," in *Le Front National à Découvert,* eds. Nonna Mayer and Pascal Perrineau. Paris: Presses de la Fondation Nationale des Science Politiques.

Mayer, Nonna and Pascal Perrineau. 1992. "Why Do They Vote for Le Pen?" *European Journal of Political Research* 22:101–121.

McKelvey, R. D. and P. C. Ordeshook. 1972. "A Theory of the Caluculus of Voting," in *Mathematical Applications in Political Science VI,* ed. J. F. Herdon and J. L. Bernd. Charlottesville: University of Virginia Press.

Mégret, Bruno. 1997. Interview by author, St. Cloud, France, October 19.

Mehrländer, Ursula. 1993. "Federal Republic of Germany: Sociological Aspects of Migration Policy," in *The Politics of Migration Policies: Settlement and Integration, the First World into the 1990s,* ed. Daniel Kubat. New York: Center for Migration Studies.

Merkl, Peter H. and Leonard Weinberg, eds. 1993. *Encounters with the Contemporary Radical Right.* Boulder, Colorado: Westview Press.

Miller, Mark J. 1981. *Foreign Workers in Western Europe.* New York: Praeger.

Milner, Susan and René Mouriaux. 1997. "France," in *The New Politics of Unemployment: Radical Policy Initiatives in Western Europe,* ed. Hugh Compston. London: Routledge.

Minkenberg, Michael. 1997. "The New Right in France and Germany: Nouvelle Droite, Neue Rechte, and the New Right Radical Parties," in *The Revival of Right-Wing Extremism in the Nineties,* ed. Peter H. Merkl and Leonard Weinberg. Portland, Oregon: Frank Cass.

_____. 1992. "The New Right in Germany: The Transformation of Conservatism and the Extreme Right." *European Journal of Political Research* 22:101–121.

_____. 1998. "The New Radical Right in the Political Process: Interaction Effects in France and Germany." Unpublished mss.

Mitra, Subrata. 1988. "The National Front in France – A Single-Issue Movement?" *West European Politics* 11 (April):47–64.

Monde, Le, dossiers et documents. 1993. *Les Elections Législatives de Mars 1993.* Paris: Le Monde.

Money, Jeannette. 1995. "Foreigners and Fanatics: Assessing the Impact of Extremist Parties on Immigration Control." Unpublished mss.

Mossuz-Lavau, Janine. 1997. "Les Comportements Electoraux," in *Institutions et Vie Politique,* ed. Jean-Luc Parodi. Paris: Documentation Française.

Mudde, Cas. 2000. *The Ideology of the Extreme Right.* Manchester: Manchester University Press.

_____. 1995. "Right-Wing Extremism Analyzed – A Comparative Analysis of the Ideologies of Three Right-wing Extremist Parties." *European Journal of Political Research* 27:203–224.

Mudde, Cas and Joop Van Holsteyn. 2000. "The Netherlands: Explaining the Limited Success of the Extreme Right," in *The Politics of the Extreme Right: From the Margins to the Mainstream,* ed. Paul Hainsworth. New York: Pinter.

Müller, Wolfgang C. 1996. "Political Parties," in *Contemporary Austrian Politics,* ed. Volkmar Lauber. Boulder, Colorado: Westview Press.

Nagle, John D. 1970. *The National Democratic Party: Right Radicalism in the Federal Republic of Germany.* Berkeley: University of California Press.

Neu, Viola. 1998. "Stagnation oder Ausdehnung? Das Potential der Rechtsparteien im Sommer 1998." Working paper, Konrad Adenauer Stiftung, Born, Germany, August.

Nickell, Stephen. 1990. "Unemployment: A Survey." *The Economic Journal* 100:391–439.

OECD – SOPEMI. 1992. *Trends in International Migration: Continuous Reporting System on Migration, Annual Report 1992.* Paris: OECD.

_____. 1994. *Trends in International Migration: Continuous Reporting System on Migration, Annual Report 1993.* Paris: OECD.

Österreichischen Statistichen Zentralamt. 1984. *Die Nationalratswahl vom 24. April 1983.* Wien: Österreichischen Statistichen Zentralamt.

Padgett, Stephen, ed. 1993. *Parties and Party Systems in the New Germany.* Brookfield, Vermont: Dartmouth Publishing.

Pelinka, Anton. 1993. *Die Kleine Koalition: SPÖ – FPÖ; 1983–1986.* Wien: Böhlau Verlag.

Pelinka, Anton and Fritz Plasser, ed. 1989. *The Austrian Party System.* Boulder, Colorado: Westview Press.

Perrineau, Pascal. 1997. *Le Symptôme Le Pen.* Paris: Fayard.

Perrineau, Pascal and Colette Ysmal. 1998. *Le Vote Surprise: Les Élections Législatives des 25 Mai et 1er Juin 1997.* Paris: Presses de Sciences Po.

Petrocik, John R. and Daron Shaw. 1991. "Nonvoting in America: Attitudes in Context," in *Political Participation and American Democracy,* ed. William Crotty. New York: Greenwood Press.

Plasser, Fritz and Peter A. Ulram 1989. "Major Parties on the Defensive: The Austrian Party and Electoral Landscape after the 1986 National Council Election" in *The Austrian Party System,* ed. Anton Pelinka/Fritz Plasser, 61–91. Boulder and London: Westview.

Plasser, Fritz, Peter A. Ulram, and Franz Sommer. 1996. "Analyse der Europawahl '96: Muster und Motive." Unpublished mss. Wien, October 14.

Plasser, Fritz, Peter A. Ulram, and Wolfgang C. Müller. 1995. *Wählerverhalten und Parteienwettbewerg: Analysen zur Nationalratswahl 1994.* Wien: Signum Verlag.

Platone, François. *Les Electorats sous la Vème République: Données d'Enquêtes 1958–1995.* Paris: Centre d'Etude de la Vie Politique Française.

Pridham, Geoffrey. 1977. *Christian Democracy in Western Germany: The CDU/CSU in Government and Opposition 1945–1976.* London: Croom Helm.

Prowe, Diethelm. 1998. "Fascism, Neo-Fascism, New Radical Right?" in *International Fascism: Theories, Causes and the New Consensus,* ed. Roger Griffin. London: Arnold.

Przeworski, Adam and Henry Teune. 1970. *The Logic of Comparative Social Inquiry.* New York: Wiley-Interscience.

Radcliffe, Benjamin. 1988. "Solving a Puzzle: Aggregate Analysis and Economic Voting Revisited." *Journal of Politics* 50:440–458.

Ritter, Gerhard. 1991. *Wahlen in Deutschland 1946–1991: Ein Handbuch.* Munich: Beck.

Roberts, Geoffrey K. 1988. "The 'Second Vote' Campaign Strategy of the West German Free Democratic Party." *European Journal of Political Research* 16:317–337.

Saalfeld, Thomas. 1993. "The Politics of National-Populism: Ideology and Policies of the German *Republikaner* Party. *German Politics* 2: 177–199.

Safran, William. 1993. "The National Front in France: From Lunatic Fringe to Limited Respectability," in *Encounters with the Contemporary Radical Right,* ed. Peter H. Merkl and Leonard Weinberg. Boulder, Colorado: Westview Press.

Sartori, Giovanni. 1997. *Comparative Constitutional Engineering: An Inquiry into Structures, Incentives and Outcomes,* 2nd ed. London: Macmillan.

Schain, Martin. 1987. "The National Front in France and the Construction of Political Legitimacy." *West European Politics* 10 (April):229–252.

———. 2000. "The Impact of the Extreme Right on Immigration Policy." Paper prepared for Conference on Explaining Changes in Migration Policies, Geneva, October 20–21.

Schlesinger, Joseph A. and Mildred S. Schlesinger. 1998. "Dual-Ballot Elections and Political Parties: The French Presidential Election of 1995." *Comparative Political Studies* 31 (February):72–97.

Schmidt, Gislher. 1968. *Ideologie und Propaganda der NPD.* Bonn: Bundeszentrale für Politische Bildung.

Schultze, Rianer-Olaf. 1995. "Voting and Non-Voting in German Elections," in *Electoral Abstention in Europe*, ed. Joan Font and Rosa Viros. Barcelona: Institut de Ciencias Polítiques i Socials.

Shields, James G. 1990. "A New Chapter in the History of the French Extreme Right: The National Front," in *French Political Parties in Transition*, ed. Alistair Cole, 185–205. Aldershot, Hampshire: Darmouth Publishing.

Simmons, Harvey G. 1996. *The French National Front: The Extremist Challenge to Democracy.* Boulder, Colorado: Westview Press.

Singer, Daniel. 1991. "The Resistible Rise of Jean-Marie Le Pen." *Ethnic and Racial Studies*, 14 (July):368–381.

Smith, Gordon. 1993. "Dimensions of Change in the German Party System," in *Parties and Party Systems in the New Germany*, ed. Stephen Padgett. Brookfield, Vermont: Darmouth Publishing.

Soysal, Yasemin N. 1994. *Limits of Citizenship: Migrants and Postnational Membership in Europe.* Chicago: University of Chicago Press.

Stevens, Anne. 1996. *The Government and Politics of France.* New York: St. Martin's Press.

Stöss, Richard. 1989. *Die Extrême Rechte in der Bundesrepublik: Entwicklung.* Opladen, Germany: Westdeutscher Verlag.

———. 1988. "The Problem of Right-Wing Extremism in West Germany." *West European Politics* 11 (April):34–46.

Strom, Kaare. 1990. *Minority Government and Majority Rule.* New York: Cambridge University Press.

Suarez-Orozco, Marcelo M. 1994. "Anxious Neighbors: Belgium and Its Immigrant Minorities," in *Controlling Immigration: A Global Perspective*, ed. Wayne A. Cornelius, Phillip L. Martin, and James F. Hollifield. Stanford: Stanford University Press.

Sully, Melanie A. 1981. *Political Parties and Elections in Austria.* London: C. Hurst.

———. 1990. *A Contemporary History of Austria.* New York: Routledge.

———. 1997. *The Haider Phenomenon.* New York: Columbia University Press.

Swank, Duane and Hans-Georg Betz. 1995. "Right Wing Populism in Western Europe." Paper presented at the 1995 annual meeting of the American Political Science Association, August 31–September 3, Chicago, Illinois.

Tarrow, Sydney. 1994. *Power in Movement: Social Movements, Collective Action and Politics.* Cambridge University Press.

Thurner, Paul W. and Franz Urban Pappi. 1998. "Measuring and Explaining Strategic Voting in the German Electoral System." Mannheimer Zentrum für Europäische Sozialforschung, Working Paper number 21, Mannheim, Germany.

———. 1999. "Causes and Effects of Coalition Preferences in a Mixed-Member Proportional System." Mannheimer Zentrum für Europäische Sozialforschung, Working Paper number 1, Mannheim, Germany.

Tsebelis, George. 1990. *Nested Games*. Berkeley: University of California Press.

Vandermotten, Christian and Jean Vanlaer. 1993. "Immigrants and the Extreme-Right Vote in Europe and in Belgium," in *Mass Migration in Europe: The Legacy and the Future*, ed. Russel King. London: Belhaven Press.

Vaughan, Michalina. 1995. "The Extreme Right in France: 'Lepénisme' or the Politics of Fear," in *The Far Right in Western and Eastern Europe*, ed. Luciano Cheles, Ronnie Ferguson, and Michalina Vaughan. New York: Longman.

Veen, Hans-Joachin, Norbert Lepszy, and Peter Mnich. 1993. *The Republikaner Party in Germany: Right-Wing Menace or Protest Catchall?* Westport, Connecticut: Praeger.

Verbunt, Gilles. 1985. "France," in *European Immigration Policy*, ed. Tomas Hammar. Cambridge: Cambridge University Press.

von Beyme, Klaus. 1988. "Right-Wing Extremism in Post-War Europe." *West European Politics* 11 (April):1–18.

von Meyer, Heino and Philippe Muheim. 1996. "Employment Is a Territorial Issue." *The OECD Observer* 203 (December 1996/January 1997):32–36.

Westle, Bettina and Oskar Niedermayer. 1992. "Contemporary Right-Wing Extremism in West Germany: The 'Republicans' and Their Electorate." *European Journal of Political Research* 22:83–100.

Widfeldt, Anders. 2000. "Scandinavia: Mixed Success for the Populist Right." *Parliamentary Affairs* 53:486–500.

Wrench, John and John Solomos. 1993. *Racism and Migration in Western Europe*. Oxford: Berg.

Ysmal, Colette. 1998. "France." *European Journal of Political Research* 34:393–401.

———. 1999. "France." *European Journal of Political Research* 36:387–393.

———. 2003. "France." *European Journal of Political Research* 42:943–956.

Zimmerman, Ekkart and Thomas Saalfeld. 1993. "The Three Waves of West German Right-Wing Extremism," in *Encounters with the Contemporary Radical Right*, ed. Peter H. Merkl and Leonard Weinberg. Boulder, Colorado: Westview Press.

Data Sources

Andersen, Johannes, Jørgen Goul Andersen, Ole Borre, and Hans Jørgen Nielsen. 1998. *Danish Electoral Survey 1998*. Copenhagen: AIM-Nielsen.

Andersen, Uwe and Wichard, Woyke. 1995. *Handwöerterbuch des politischen Systems der Bundesrepublik Deutschland*, 2. Auflage. Opladen: Leske und Budrich.

Dachs, Herbert. 1992. *Parteien und Wahlen in Österreichs Bundesländern 1945–1991*. Munchen: R. Oldenbourg Verlag.

Dumartin, Sylvie. "L'Evolution du Taux de Chômage dans les Départements de 1987 à 1990." *INSEE PREMIERE 154* (July 1991).

———. "Le Géographie du Chômage en 1991." *INSEE PREMIERE 227* (September 1992).

———. "Le Chômage Régional et Départmental en 1992." *INSEE PREMIERE 283* (October 1993).

FESSEL-Gfk. 1999. *Election Exit Poll*. Vienna: FESSEL-Gfk.

Forschungsgruppe Wahlen (Institute for Election Research). 1995. *Politbarometer West [Germany], 1977–1995, Partial Accumulation*. Cologne, Germany: Central Archive for Empirical Social Research.

Infomedia. http://www.polinfo.dk/infomedia/MainPage.aspx?pageid = / informedia/forside.ascx.Copenhagen: Infomedia.

Institut National de la Statistiques et des Études Économiques. 1996. *Tableaux de l'Economie Française*. Paris: INSEE.

———. 1962, 1968, 1975, 1982, 1990. *Recensement général de la population*. Paris: INSEE.

LexisNexis® Academic. http://web.lexis-nexis.com/universe. New York: Reed-Elsevier.

Marchand, Olivier and Christine Monceau. "Taux de Chomage Nationaux, Régionaux et Départementaux." *Collections de L'INSEE: Premiers Resultats 85* (February 1987).

Marchand, Olivier and Nicole Marc. "Taux de Chomage Nationaux, Régionaux et Départementaux." *Collections de L'INSEE: Premiers Resultats 118* (February 1988).

OECD. 1960–1997. *Labour Force Statistics*. Paris: OECD.

OECD-SOPEMI. 1992. *Trends in International Migration: Continuous Reporting System on Migration, Annual Report 1992*. Paris: OECD.

———. 1994. *Trends in International Migration: Continuous Reporting System on Migration, Annual Report 1993*. Paris: OECD.

Österreichischen Statistischen Zentralamt. 1960, 1962, 1963, 1966, 1968, 1970, 1972, 1975, 1976, 1980, 1981, 1985, 1986, 1987, 1990, 1995. *Statistisches Jahrbuch für die Republik Österreich*. Wien: Österreichischen Statistischen Zentralamt.

———.1964. *Volkszählungergebnisse 1961 – Heft 13, Heft 17*. Wien: Österreichischen Statistischen Zentralamt.

———. 1974. *Volkszählungergebnisse 1971 – Ausländer*. Wien: Österreichischen Statistischen Zentralamt.

———. 1984. *Volkszählungergebnisse 1981 – Hauptergebnisse I Österreich*. Wien: Österreichischen Statistischen Zentralamt, 1984.

———. 1985. *Volkszählungergebnisse 1981 – Hauptergebnisse II Österreich*. Wien: Österreichischen Statistischen Zentralamt.

———. 1993. *Volkszählungergebnisse 1991 – Hauptergebnisse I und II Österreich*. Wien: Österreichischen Statistischen Zentralamt.

Reif, Karlheinz and Anna Melich. 1991. *Eurobarometer 30: Immigrants and Out-Groups in Western Europe, October–November 1988* [computer file]. Conducted by Faits et Opinions, Paris. ECPSR edition. Ann Arbor, Michigan: Inter University Consortium for Political and Social Research Producer and Distributor.

———. 1993. *Eurobarometer 35: Foreign Relations, the Common Agricultural Policy and Environmental Concerns*, Spring 1991 [computer file]. Conducted by INRA (Europe), Brussels. ECPSR edition. Koeln, Germany: Zentralarchiv fuer empirische Sozialforschung and Ann Arbor, Michigan: Inter University Consortium for Political and Social Research.

———. 1993. *Eurobarometer 37* [computer file]. Conducted by INRA (Europe), Brussels. ECPSR edition. Koeln, Germany: Zentralarchiv für Empirische Sozialforschung and Ann Arbor, Michigan: Inter University Consortium for Political and Social Research.

———. 1993. *Eurobarometer 39*, Spring 1991 [computer file]. Conducted by INRA (Europe), Brussels. ECPSR edition. Koeln, Germany: Zentralarchiv für Empirische Sozialforschung and Ann Arbor, Michigan: Inter University Consortium for Political and Social Research.

SOFRES. 1988. *Post-Electoral Survey*. Paris: SOFRES.

———. 1997. *Local Press Group Survey*, March 5–7 1997. Paris: SOFRES.

SOFRES, CEVIPOF (Centre d'Etudes de la Vie Politique Française). 1997. *Post-Electoral Survey*. Paris: SOFRES.

Statistisches Bundesamt. 1961, 1962, 1963, 1965, 1967, 1969, 1970, 1973, 1975, 1976, 1991, 1994, 1995. *Statistisches Jahrbuch für die Bundesrepublik Deutschland*. Stuttgart: W. Kohlhammer.

————. 1962, 1965, 1967, 1970, 1976. *Bevölkerungsstruktur und Wirtschaftskraft der Bundesländer.* Stuttgart: W. Kohlhammer.

————. 1989. *Bevölkerungsstruktur und Erwerbstätigkeit: Volkszählung vom 25 Mai 1987, Heft 5: Struktur der Ausländischen Bevölkerung.* Stuttgart: Metzler Poeschel.

————. 1996. *Bevölkerungsstruktur und Wirtschaftskraft der Bundesländer.* Stuttgart: Metzler Poeschel.

Party Documents

AUSTRIA

FPÖ. "Bündnis für Arbeit." Vienna: FPÖ, 1997.

FRANCE

Front National. *300 Mésures pour la Renaissance de la France*. Paris: Éditions Nationales, 1993.
Parti Socialiste. *Rapport d'Orientation pour un Combat Efficace du Parti Socialiste contre le Front National*. March 1997. Paris.
Rassemblement pour la République, Union pour la Démocratie Française. *Plateformes*. 1978, 1981, 1986, 1993, 1997. Paris.

GERMANY

Christlich Demokratische Union Deutschlands. *Wahlanalyse*. 1962, 1965, 1972, 1983, 1986, 1987. Bonn.
_____. *Wahlprogramm*. 1969, 1972, 1976, 1980, 1983, 1987, 1990, 1994. Bonn.
_____. *Berliner Programm*. 1971. Bonn.
_____. *Die CDU-Parteiprogramme: eine Dokumentation der Ziele und Aufgaben,* ed. Peter Hintze. Bonn: Bouvier, 1995.
Freie Demokratische Partei. *Aufruf der Freien Demokratischen Partei zur Bundestagswahl 1961*. 1961. Bonn.
_____. *Die Bundestagswahl 1972: Ihre Bedeutung für die FDP*. April 26, 1973. Bonn.
_____. *Wahlprogramm*. 1976, 1980, 1983, 1994. Bonn.
_____. *Analyse der Bundestagswahl 1980*. November 1980. Bonn.
_____. *Karlsruher Entwurf*. June 1996. Bonn.

Konrad Adenauer Stiftung – CDU Press Archives. 1962, 1965, 1969, 1972, 1976, 1980, 1983, 1987, 1990. Bonn.
Nationaldemokratische Partei Deutschlands. *Programm.* 1967, 1973. Bonn.
Die Republikaner. *Parteiprogramm.* 1990, 1993, 1995. Bonn.
———. *Berliner Programm 1995.* Berlin: Republikaner, 1995.
Die Republikaner, Baden-Württemberg. *Ignoranz, Arroganz und Menschenverachtung.* Stuttgart. 1996.
Sozialedemokratische Partei Deutschlands. *Wahlprogramme.* 1961, 1965, 1969, 1972, 1980, 1983, 1987, 1990, 1994. Bonn.
———. *Die Bundestagswahl 1965.* 1965. Bonn.
———. *Zur Auseinandersetzung mit der NPD.* 1968. Bonn.
———. *Bundestagswahlkampf 1972.* 1972. Bonn.
———. *Die Bundestagswahlkampf 1976.* 1976. Bonn.
———. *Die Bundestagswahl vom 27.1.1987 – Analyse and Konsequenzen.* 1987. Bonn.
———. *Wahlkampf 1990.* 1990. Bonn.
———. Press documentation. 1990, 1994. Bonn.
———. *Die REP im Vorwahlkampf 1993.* Bonn.
———. *Der Wahlkampfauftakt der "Republikaner"* August 1993. Bonn.
———. *10 Punkte zur Sozialdemokratischen Auseinandersetzung mit Rechtsextremisten in den Wahlkämpfen 1994.* Bonn.
———. *Die Sogenannten "Republikaner" – Eine Rechtsextreme Chaospartei.* April 1994. Bonn.
———. *Die REP: Eine Rechtsextreme Chaospartei.* May 1994. Bonn.

DENMARK

People's Party. 2001. "Political Programme." Available at http://www.danskfolkeparti.dk/dgcm/show.as?parent=14921. Accessed July 9, 2001.
Progress Party. 2001. "The Progress Party and the Treaty of Amsterdam." Available at http://www.fremskridtspartiet.dk/foreign/engelsk2.htm. Accessed March 11, 2004.

Index